WORLD HISTORY SERIES

The Islamic Empire

by
Phyllis Corzine

LUCENT BOOKS

An imprint of Thomson Gale, a part of The Thomson Corporation

THOMSON

™

GALE

Detroit • New York • San Francisco • San Diego • New Haven, Conn. • Waterville, Maine • London • Munich

For more information, contact
Lucent Books
27500 Drake Rd.
Farmington Hills, MI 48331-3535
Or you can visit our Internet site at http://www.gale.com

LIBRARY OF CONGRESS CATALOGING-IN-PUBLICATION DATA

Corzine, Phyllis, 1943–
    The Islamic Empire / by Phyllis Corzine.
        p. cm. — (World history series)
    Includes bibliographical references and index.
    ISBN 1-59018-371-1 (hardcover : alk. paper)
    1. Islamic Empire—Juvenile literature. 2. Civilization, Islamic—Juvenile literature.
I. Title. II. Series: World history series
    DS38.3.C67 2004
    909'.09767—dc22

                                                                    2004010853

Printed in the United States of America

Contents

Foreword

Each year on the first day of school, nearly every history teacher faces the task of explaining why his or her students should study history. One logical answer to this question is that exploring what happened in our past explains how the things we often take for granted—our customs, ideas, and institutions—came to be. As statesman and historian Winston Churchill put it, "Every nation or group of nations has its own tale to tell. Knowledge of the trials and struggles is necessary to all who would comprehend the problems, perils, challenges, and opportunities which confront us today." Thus, a study of history puts modern ideas and institutions in perspective. For example, though the founders of the United States were talented and creative thinkers, they clearly did not invent the concept of democracy. Instead, they adapted some democratic ideas that had originated in ancient Greece and with which the Romans, the British, and others had experimented. An exploration of these cultures, then, reveals their very real connection to us through institutions that continue to shape our daily lives.

Another reason often given for studying history is the idea that lessons exist in the past from which contemporary societies can benefit and learn. This idea, although controversial, has always been an intriguing one for historians. Those who agree that society can benefit from the past often quote philosopher George Santayana's famous statement, "Those who cannot remember the past are condemned to repeat it." Historians who subscribe to Santayana's philosophy believe that, for example, studying the events that led up to the major world wars or other significant historical events would allow society to chart a different and more favorable course in the future.

Just as difficult as convincing students of the importance of studying history is the search for useful and interesting supplementary materials that present historical events in a context that can be easily understood. The volumes in Lucent Books' World History Series attempt to present a broad, balanced, and penetrating view of the march of history. Ancient Egypt's important wars and rulers, for example, are presented against the rich and colorful backdrop of Egyptian religious, social, and cultural developments. The series engages the reader by enhancing historical events with these cultural contexts. For example, in *Ancient Greece*, the text covers the role of women in that society. Slavery is discussed in *The Roman Empire*, as well as how slaves earned their freedom. The numerous and varied aspects of everyday life in these and other societies are explored in each volume of the series. Additionally, the series covers the major political, cultural, and philosophical ideas as the torch of civilization is passed from ancient Mesopotamia and Egypt, through Greece, Rome, Medieval Europe, and other world cultures, to the modern day.

The material in the series is formatted in a thorough, precise, and organized manner.

Each volume offers the reader a comprehensive and clearly written overview of an important historical event or period. The topic under discussion is placed in a broad, historical context. For example, *The Italian Renaissance* begins with a discussion of the High Middle Ages and the loss of central control that allowed certain Italian cities to develop artistically. The book ends by looking forward to the Reformation and interpreting the societal changes that grew out of the Renaissance. Thus, students are not only involved in an historical era, but also enveloped by the events leading up to that era and the events following it.

One important and unique feature in the World History Series is the primary and secondary source quotations that richly supplement each volume. These quotes are useful in a number of ways. First, they allow students access to sources they would not normally be exposed to because of the difficulty and obscurity of the original source. The quotations range from interesting anecdotes to farsighted cultural perspectives and are drawn from historical witnesses both past and present. Second, the quotes demonstrate how and where historians themselves derive their information on the past as they strive to reach a consensus on historical events. Lastly, all of the quotes are footnoted, familiarizing students with the citation process and allowing them to verify quotes and/or look up the original source if the quote piques their interest.

Finally, the books in the World History Series provide a detailed launching point for further research. Each book contains a bibliography specifically geared toward student research. A second, annotated bibliography introduces students to all the sources the author consulted when compiling the book. A chronology of important dates gives students an overview, at a glance, of the topic covered. Where applicable, a glossary of terms is included.

In short, the series is designed not only to acquaint readers with the basics of history, but also to make them aware that their lives are a part of an ongoing human saga. Perhaps then they will come to the same realization as famed historian Arnold Toynbee. In his monumental work, *A Study of History*, he wrote about becoming aware of history flowing through him in a mighty current, and of his own life "welling like a wave in the flow of this vast tide."

Important Dates in the History of the Islamic Empire

622
The Hegira, in which Muhammad and his followers move from Mecca to Medina.

632
Muhammad dies.

642
Muslims gain control of the Persian Empire.

656–661
The reign of Ali, the last of the "Rightly Guided" caliphs.

661–750
The Umayyad dynasty.

610
Muhammad receives his first revelation and begins preaching.

| 500 | 600 | 620 | 640 | 660 | 680 |

610–733
Islam spreads across Arabia, southern Europe, North Africa, and Asia to India.

661
The Umayyads establish their capital in Damascus.

570
The prophet Muhammad is born.

630
The Muslims conquer Mecca.

644–656
The reign of Caliph Uthman.

680
Husayn is killed at the Battle of Karbala.

634–644
The reign of Caliph Umar, the greatest period of conquests by Arabs.

632–634
The reign of Caliph Abu Bakr; the Riddah Wars occur.

691
The Mosque of Umar
(Dome of the Rock)
is built in Jerusalem.

732
Charles Martel defeats
Muslims at Tours and
stops the Muslim
advance into Europe.

1099
Jerusalem is
captured by the
crusaders.

750–1258
The Abbasid
dynasty.

1097
The first crusaders
reach Syria.

892
The capital is
returned to
Baghdad.

1055
Seljuk Turks
capture
Baghdad.

| 700 | 800 | 900 | 1000 | 1100 | 1200 |

711–713
The
Muslims
conquer
Spain.

1187
Saladin defeats
the crusaders
and captures
Jerusalem.

945
The Buwayids take
control of the caliphate.

836
With the introduction of
Turkish mercenaries, the
capital is moved from
Baghdad to Samarra.

762
The Abbasids
move the capital
from Damascus to
Baghdad.

1258
Mongols sack
Baghdad and kill
the last Abbasid
caliph.

786–809
The reign of Caliph
Harun ar-Rashid;
the Islamic Empire
is at the peak of its
golden age.

An Empire That Changed the World

Some fourteen hundred years ago, while western Europe languished in the Dark Ages, the deserts of Arabia gave birth to a remarkable empire. Within the space of a decade, Arab warriors, motivated by a new religion, Islam (and the desire for treasure), conquered what are now Syria, Palestine, Egypt, and most of Iraq. In a little over a century, they built an empire that spanned substantial parts of three continents—Africa, Asia, and Europe—displacing the older civilizations of the Byzantines to the west and the Persian Sassanids in the east.

The empire created by the warriors of Allah (the Arabic word for God) was greater than the Roman Empire at its height; it stretched from Spain and Portugal in the west to the borders of India and China in the east. In the course of its expansion, the Islamic Empire brought its religion and its language to people of a multitude of ethnic backgrounds, religions, and languages. Not the Roman, British, or Russian empires—or any empire before or since—assimilated such a diverse population. According to scholar Albert Hourani, the Islamic Empire

had a unity which transcended divisions of time and space; the Arabic language could open the door to office and influence throughout the world; a body of knowledge, transmitted over the centuries by a known chain of teachers, preserved a moral community even when rulers changed; places of pilgrimage, Mecca and Jerusalem, were unchanging poles of the human world even if power shifted from one city to another.[1]

Arabs built on the ancient civilizations of Babylonia and Egypt, of which they were heirs, and absorbed elements of Greek and Roman cultures. The Arabs and those they conquered preserved and drew on the knowledge of all these ancient peoples to create a dazzling civilization that became one of the grandest achievements of humankind. Though the Arab people were the first warriors and founders of the Islamic state, other peoples were absorbed into the empire and helped build Islamic civilization. The Persians were especially

An Islamic holy man calls people to prayer from atop a mosque. During the seventh century, Arab warriors spread the religion of Islam throughout the Middle East.

important contributors to Islamic civilization.

Islamic scholars, mathematicians, and scientists gathered in magnificent cities, where they studied and translated ancient Greek texts. Artists and artisans helped build ornate palaces, houses of worship, public baths, libraries, and other public buildings. Weavers created fine textiles, known today by names such as muslin and taffeta. Artisans created the process for making that most delicate glassware—crystal. And scholars passed on the heritage of the Koran (or Qur'an), Islam's holy book, in Islamic schools, or madrassas.

Even though the Islamic Empire remained misunderstood and feared by Europeans of the Middle Ages, this great empire helped shape western Europe, and its influence is still felt today. Islamic scholars translated the works of the ancient Greeks and Romans, preserving texts that might otherwise have been lost for all time. To some measure, then, the West owes the great rebirth and flowering of culture known as the Renaissance to these Islamic scholars. These scholars and scientists also made their own contributions to disciplines such as medicine, astronomy, and mathematics. An Islamic mathematician developed the branch of mathematics known as algebra (from the Arabic word *al-jabr*). The medical text written by the Islamic scientist Ibn Sina (known to Europeans as Avicenna) was used in European medical schools until the seventeenth century. Islamic scientists were also responsible for establishing chemistry and pharmacology as sciences.

No less a contribution to the world was the religion of Islam. From its remote beginnings in the Arabian Peninsula, Islam was spread by the warriors of Allah and became the foundation on which the empire was built. Islam has provided spiritual inspiration and comfort to billions of people over the centuries and to this day remains a way of life for millions of people around the globe.

The Arabic language is another enduring contribution of the Islamic Empire. For centuries, the Arabic language was the language of culture and learning. During the Middle Ages, the most important works of philosophy, medicine, history, and astronomy were produced in Arabic. Today, over 100 million people speak Arabic as their native language, and because the Koran is written in Arabic, millions of others use the language as they recite their daily prayers.

During the Islamic Empire, the Muslims (the name by which the followers of Islam refer to themselves) built widespread trade routes from one end of the empire to the other. By this means, luxury goods such as spices, fine textiles, and porcelain found their way to Europeans. To make exchange easier, Arab traders invented the "letter of credit," or check, which could be exchanged for goods almost anywhere in the empire.

The changes brought by the Islamic Empire echo through the centuries since its fall. The religion and language of the empire still unify millions of people, and the fruits of that empire's intellectual contributions are enjoyed by people throughout the world today.

1 The Birth of Islam

The great Islamic Empire arose out of an improbable setting—the Arabian Peninsula—over 1 million square miles of sparsely populated desert and steppes, dotted with oases and edged with a narrow strip of cultivatable land. This vast desert peninsula, which today is home to the modern nations of Saudi Arabia, Kuwait, Yemen, the United Arab Emirates, Oman, and Qatar, was mostly inhabited by tribes of wandering nomads called the Bedouin, whose way of life made unified action unlikely. Yet it was these Bedouin who embraced the religion of Islam. In the words of Umar, an early Islamic ruler, the Bedouin "furnished Islam with its raw material."[2]

THE LAND AND CLIMATE OF THE ARABIAN PENINSULA

The Bedouin's knowledge of the world extended little beyond the Arabian Desert, which covers the great central portion of the peninsula, and penetrates northward into the modern-day nations of Syria, Jordan, and Iraq. To the east of the peninsula lies the Persian Gulf; to the west, the Red Sea and Nile Valley; and to the south, the Arabian Sea and Indian Ocean. The Arabs gave this huge desert the name *Jazirat al-Arab*, the "Island of the Arabs."

The Arabian Peninsula's climate was—and is—one of the hottest and driest in the world. It varies, however, from north to south. In the north, the coast receives a little rain, and the interior receives practically no rain at all. Except for the small settlements around the widely scattered oases and towns in larger oases, few people lived in the region. In the south, the climate is much more hospitable, and the region receives enough rainfall to be a center of agriculture, producing coffee, herbs, and spices. Traders carrying the agricultural goods of the south had to pass through the wasteland of the rest of Arabia to reach trade centers in the north. From ancient times, north Arabia monopolized the trade routes, not only those to the south but those to the Persian Gulf and Indian Ocean as well.

PEOPLE OF ARABIA: THE BEDOUIN

The Bedouin of the sixth century A.D. had little in the way of material wealth other than their livestock, yet this lack of wordly

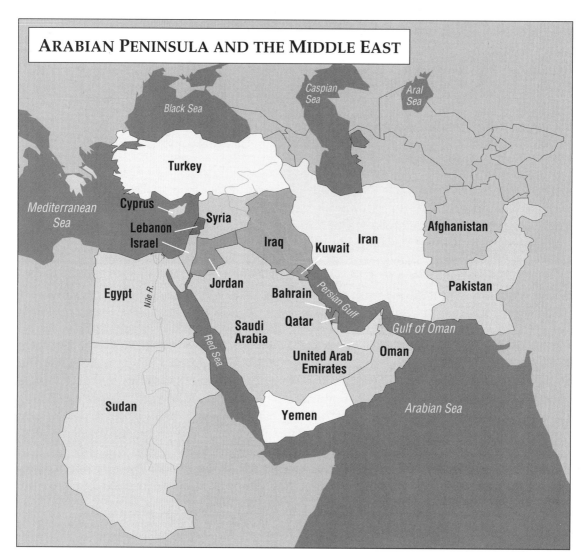

ARABIAN PENINSULA AND THE MIDDLE EAST

goods suited them. Scholar F.E. Peters says of the Bedouin:

> The nomadic tribes of the steppe lived off their camel and sheep herds, their horse breeding and their raiding the property of others. It was a [difficult] existence at best, but in the minds of the Bedouin infinitely superior to that of the agricultural peasant with his mean plot. The farmer knew neither chivalry nor *asabiyah* [group solidarity]; he was a slave to his garden, his political masters and his gods. All these sat lightly upon the Bedouin who found his fulfillment in the comradeship of dangers shared and challenges met. He had his freedom and his clan, and both are faithfully mirrored in the poetry that was his chief entertainment and his principal legacy.[3]

In addition to the Bedouin, the Arabian Peninsula was home to people who lived in small settlements and worked as farmers, craftsmen, or merchants. The line between the sedentary townspeople and villagers and the Bedouin was not always firm, since some townspeople had been nomads at one time. Moreover, the Bedouin relied on the towns and farming villages for foods they could not produce themselves and for other necessities. The Bedouin traded their livestock, milk and milk products, and animal hides for goods such as cloth, weapons, and metal products.

Although the Bedouin were a minority of the population, their tribal leaders exercised a great deal of political control in the region. The Bedouin had close ties with the merchants whose caravans passed through Bedouin territory. These merchants relied on the oases controlled by the Bedouin as places to water their pack animals and replenish their supplies.

During the sixth century, tribes of wandering nomads called the Bedouin roamed the Middle East, living off their camel and sheep herds.

Thus the two groups—the Bedouin and merchants—had strong bonds of mutual interest. Together they dominated the farmers and craftsmen, who relied on the merchants to sell or transport what they produced.

Some Bedouin tribes were also able to maintain power by controlling religious sanctuaries. According to Hourani,

> Gods were thought of as dwelling in a sanctuary, a *haram*, a place or town set apart from tribal conflict, serving as a centre of pilgrimage, sacrifice, meeting and arbitration, and watched over by a family under the protection of a neighbouring tribe. Such a family could obtain power or influence by making skilful use of its religious prestige, its role as arbiter of tribal disputes, and its opportunities for trade.[4]

Members of religiously powerful tribes served as guardians of the local god's shrine, or *haram*. Translated into English, *haram* means "sanctuary." The family enforced rules against murder and other types of violence. Members of feuding tribes knew that in these market towns they could visit the shrines of their gods and not fear attack from their enemies. The *harams* also usually had a cult leader who served as an arbitrator, peacemaker, and judge. This leader had the authority to settle disputes among feuding warrior tribes. Thus the *haram* was a center of peace where the rule of law was observed. This peace allowed the *haram* to become a center for trade as well, which in turn helped the family of religious guardians grow in power and wealth.

THE BASIS OF BEDOUIN SOCIETY

Blood relationships—the ties to the tribe and clan—were the basis of Bedouin society and of Bedouin justice. If a clan member murdered a fellow clan member, the murderer became an outcast. If a clan member murdered someone outside his clan, however, then a blood feud was created, and only the death of a member of the murderer's clan could settle the score. As scholar Philip Hitti explains, "Blood, according to the primitive law of the desert, calls for blood; no [punishment] is recognized other than that of vengeance."[5]

The tribal chief was responsible for taking care of the tribe, leading migrations, and extending hospitality to outsiders, and often—though not always—he was the war leader. He led by his influence and standing within the tribe. Succession to the chiefdom was not inherited, although chiefs usually came from the same families, and some "great families" enjoyed an aristocratic status among other tribes. In general, though, the Bedouin had little regard for authority. As al-Qutami, an eighth-century Arab writer, noted, "At one time we obey our [chief], and then another time we disobey him; we do not feel ourselves bound to seek his counsel all the time."[6]

The Bedouin tribes, moreover, were autonomous. Although they made alliances with one another, these alliances were easily broken. There were divisions among tribes of north and central Arabia, and the tribes often warred with each other. However, the tribes enjoyed a certain internal unity and were bound together in a hierarchical order of the greater and lesser families.

Saharan nomads face Mecca during the evening prayer. Mecca has been an important religious center since biblical times.

THE MOST IMPORTANT CITIES

For the people of central and north Arabia the two most important cities were Mecca and Medina. Mecca lies in the south of a range of coastal mountains known as the Hejaz, in a dusty, rocky, barren valley. The name *Mecca* means "sanctuary," and the city was an important religious center even as early as biblical times. According to tradition, the biblical patriarch Abraham visited his son Ishmael at Mecca, where he drank at the well of Zamzam, located on the city's outskirts. Mecca was the site of the Ka'bah, a cube-shaped building where the Bedouin came to worship and make sacrifices to pagan deities. The Ka'bah housed many statues of idols and was home to many gods, including one known as Allah. The custodians of the Ka'bah were the powerful tribe known as the Quraysh, who were also important merchants and traders of Mecca.

Besides being a religious center, Mecca was a trading town. Mecca was the approximate midway point on the long caravan route between Yemen in the south and the northern trade centers of Gaza and Damascus in Syria. Mecca's strategic location and its status as a sanctuary made it the most important city in the Hejaz. The significance of the Meccan trade is described by Peters:

> Single caravans did not pass from the Yemen to Syria; it was, rather, the Meccans who annually sent their own caravans of a thousand camels to both the northern and the southern [trade centers]. Thus it was the Meccans and their [most powerful] tribe of the Quraysh who were the unique entrepreneurs of the Arabian trade.[7]

About three hundred miles to the north of Mecca lies the city of Medina, originally known as Yathrib. Like Mecca, Medina was an important location on the caravan route. But unlike Mecca, Medina was in an oasis well suited for agriculture, especially for growing the date palm, a staple of the Arabian diet.

This was the land from which a great empire would arise: a few widely scattered settlements dominated by nomadic tribesmen. These nomads, well armed, unafraid of shedding blood, and fiercely loyal to their tribes, were capable of great conquests—if only someone were able to unite them.

THE PROPHET MUHAMMAD

That individual was a well-respected merchant of Mecca known as Muhammad. He was a spiritual person who frequently meditated alone in a cave outside Mecca. In the year A.D. 610, when Muhammad was forty years old, he received his calling. One day, while meditating in a cave, he heard a voice commanding:

Recite! In the name of your Lord who
  created,
Who created men from clotted blood.
Recite! Your Lord is the most beneficent,
Who taught by the pen,
Taught to men what they did not know.[8]

This revelation would be the first of many Muhammad received over the next twenty-two years. Muhammad believed that these revelations were from God and were transmitted, or spoken, by the angel Gabriel. The message Muhammad heard was much the same as that spoken by the ancient Hebrew prophets: There is only one God, all-powerful, creator of the universe. There will be a final judgment day. Those who obey the commands of God will earn the rewards of paradise, while those who disobey them will suffer the pains of hell.

Muhammad's wife Khadijah was the first to accept his revelations as genuine. According to Muhammad's biographer, she told him, "By Him in whose hand is Khadija's soul, I hope that thou wilt be the prophet of His people."[9] Gradually Muhammad gathered a small group of believers, some of whom were younger members of the most influential clans of

A painting depicts the prophet Muhammad being visited by the angel Gabriel. His face is obscured out of respect for Islamic tradition.

the tribe of Quraysh. His followers called themselves Muslims, an Arabic word meaning "those who surrender to God."

THE HEGIRA

As Muhammad's influence grew, the elders of Quraysh came to regard Muhammad as attacking their way of life. They were the guardians of the Ka'bah, the sanctuary at Mecca. Muhammad claimed that the many gods they worshipped in the Ka'bah were false and that there was only one true God. According to Muhammad's biographer, the Quraysh leaders appealed to Muhammad's uncle, Abu Talib, who was Muhammad's supporter and protector among them: "O Abu Talib, your nephew has cursed our gods, insulted our religion, mocked our way of life, and accused our forefathers of error."[10]

Both Khadijah and Abu Talib died in the year 619. Grieved by these losses and facing growing opposition to his teachings, Muhammad decided to leave Mecca. Muhammad had a reputation of being a fair and skilled arbitrator, and so when he was invited to the town that later became known as Medina to help settle a quarrel between two competing tribal alliances, he accepted. In 622 Muhammad and his followers moved to Medina. Those who followed him to Medina became known as the Emigrants or the companions. Following Muhammad and leaving Mecca was an important act of faith for these people. They left behind their tribal and family ties and their livelihoods to create a new community based not on tribal loyalties but on religious faith. Later generations would date the beginning of the Islamic era and the first year of the Islamic calendar from this move, which became known as the Hegira.

The people of Medina welcomed Muhammad, and he made many converts and established a community—the *ummah*, or community of Islam. The *ummah* replaced the tribe and clan that had been the primary bonds for people. In the *ummah*, Muhammad's message was law. This new law provided for sweeping changes in his followers' lifestyles. Muhammad outlawed the worship of idols, and he forbade the drinking of wine and the eating of pork. He limited the number of wives a man could have and limited divorce. He also placed regulations on the way masters were to treat their slaves.

As radical as these changes were, Muhammad believed that his role was that of reformer, not a prophet of a new religion. He believed that over time the prophecies given to Jews and Christians had been altered and corrupted. His message returned to the first pure revelation intended by God.

Muhammad's message was accepted by more and more people, and as his influence grew and spread throughout the region, the Meccans became angry and finally went to war against him. Although they attacked Medina several times, Muhammad's followers managed to repel them in a series of bloody battles. His followers were badly outnumbered but fought bravely, believing that God was with them. They were nearly wiped out, but Bedouin tribesmen, hearing of the courage of these fighters, joined the fight on their side. Finally, in 630 Muhammad

THE KORAN

The revelations or recitations that were given to Muhammad by the angel Gabriel were gathered by others into the holy book the Koran. Each revelation is called a sura, which begins with Muhammad's own words: "In the name of Allah, the Compassionate, the Merciful."

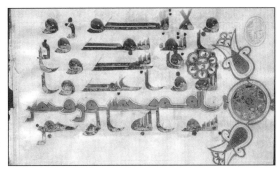

Part of the power of Muhammad's message was the very language in which it was delivered. To the Arabs, who appreciated the beauty of their spoken language, these revelations were more beautiful than any poetry.

Pictured is a page from a ninth-century manuscript of the Koran.

succeeded in overcoming the Meccans, and he entered the city of Mecca in triumph. Rather than punish the people of Mecca, he pardoned them, an extraordinary act of mercy for the time. Muhammad then entered the Ka'bah and destroyed the many idols there, proclaiming, "Truth hath come, and falsehood hath vanished."[11] The holy sanctuary of Mecca became the center of the Islamic world. Muhammad directed all devout Muslims to face in the direction of Mecca as they recite their daily prayers.

Muhammad went on to earn the loyalty of the many tribes of Arabia and convert them to Islam. The tribes paid the *zakat*, or poor tax, which was used to help the poor of their tribe. Gradually, Muhammad was uniting the tribes of Arabia and beginning to build an Islamic state.

After his conquest of Mecca, Muhammad lived only two more years. He died in Medina in 632 and was buried there in what became known as the Prophet's Mosque. He left behind a religion that would be the foundation of an empire. With Islam, Muhammad established the *ummah*, the community of believers—not tribal membership—as the primary bond. In his own words:

> O ye men! Hearken unto my words and take ye them to heart! Know ye that every Moslem is a brother unto every other Moslem, and that ye are now one brotherhood. It is not legitimate for any one of you, therefore, to appropriate unto himself anything that belongs to his brother unless it is willingly given him by that brother.[12]

Thus the stage was set for Islamic expansion throughout the known world.

THE APPEAL OF ISLAM

This idea of equality naturally appealed to the independent and freedom-loving Bedouin. Muhammad condemned the excessive accumulation of wealth and class inequality, ideas that appealed to the poor and to slaves. In addition, Muhammad preached that all men were brothers within a social order established by God. The master was no better than the slave in the eyes of Allah. Those who belonged to clan and tribe and those who were outcasts, orphans, or without alliances knelt together in prayer and had an equal claim to paradise. People from all levels of society, and from every region of the known world, were equals.

Muhammad taught that the practice of Islam is based on Five Pillars: bearing witness, prayer, almsgiving, fasting, and the hajj, or pilgrimage to Mecca. In the year 632, Muhammad himself led the hajj to Mecca. Thereafter his journey became

A fourteenth-century Turkish painting shows Muhammad addressing an army outside Mecca. Muhammad's followers conquered the city in the year 630.

THE FIVE PILLARS OF ISLAM

Most important to the practice of Islam is the observance of what is known as the Five Pillars of Islam. The first pillar is *shahada*, or the "act of bearing witness." Bearing witness consists of saying "There is no God but Allah, and Muhammad is his Prophet." This simple assertion is all that is required to become a Muslim.

The second pillar is *salat*, or prayer, which is the Muslim's most important act of devotion to God. Muslims pray five times a day: at daybreak, noon, midafternoon, after sunset, and during the evening. A crier, or muezzin, calls the faithful to prayer at the prescribed times. Before prayers, Muslims engage in a ritual ablution, or washing. During prayer, Muslims face the city of Mecca and go through a prescribed series of physical movements—kneeling, bowing, sitting, and standing—and recitations of prescribed verses from the Koran in the original Arabic. On Fridays, Muslims gather in a group to recite their noon prayers, often in a mosque. A religious leader called an imam delivers a short sermon at the Friday prayers.

Almsgiving, or *zakat*, is the third pillar of Islam, and is required of all devout Muslims. They give a percentage of their wealth each year for the benefit of those in need, and they believe that such almsgiving not only benefits the needy but also "purifies" their wealth.

The fourth pillar of Islam is fasting during the month in the Islamic calendar known as Ramadan. The Koran instructs all Muslims to fast during Ramadan (with the exception of the sick, injured, pregnant and nursing women, and the elderly). From sunrise to sunset, Muslims completely abstain from food, drink, smoking, and sexual relations. After sunset, they resume normal activities. The purpose of fasting is to practice self-restraint, spiritual reflection, and obedience to God.

Pilgrimage is the fifth pillar of Islam. The Koran requires all Muslims who are able to make a pilgrimage, or hajj, to the Ka'bah in the Great Mosque at Mecca to do so once in their lifetime.

known as the "Pilgrimage of Farewell." Muhammad's followers used the details of what turned out to be his final pilgrimage as a model for ritual for all the future generations of pilgrims.

Shortly after Muhammad returned to Medina from the hajj, he came down with a fever. His illness worsened, and he died ten days later, at age sixty-two. His death occurred twenty-two years after the angel Gabriel had first spoken to him. The legacy Muhammad left would soon spread like a firestorm across the Middle East and beyond.

2 Building the Empire

Within a little more than a decade following the death of Muhammad, Arab warriors had established Islamic rule not just on the Arabian Peninsula but throughout Iraq, Persia, Syria, Egypt, and North Africa. The speed with which Islam spread astonished observers at that time. As historian Philip Hitti explains,

> If someone in the first third of the seventh Christian century had had the audacity to prophesy that within a decade some unheralded, unforeseen power from the hitherto barbarous and little known land of Arabia was to make its appearance, hurl itself against the only two world powers of the age, fall heir to the one—the Sasanid [or Persian]—and strip the other—the Byzantine—of its fairest provinces, he would undoubtedly have been declared a lunatic. Yet that was exactly what happened.[13]

ABU BAKR, THE FIRST CALIPH

The death of Muhammad left his followers in crisis. Who, they wondered, could take his place? On hearing of the death of Muhammad, Abu Bakr, the Prophet's oldest and closest friend and supporter, stepped forward to reassure the people that the religion of Islam would continue.

But what, Muslims asked, would come of the new Islamic state that Muhammad had been in the process of building? Muhammad had been not only the spiritual leader but the political leader, or head of state, as well. Now with Muhammad's death, the political unity he had built among the tribes of the Arabian Peninsula began to crumble. Finding a leader who could restore that unity was a problem, however.

Those people in Medina who had welcomed Muhammad and helped spread his teachings believed that a leader should be chosen from among their own number. Another group, the Emigrants or the Companions of the Flight, had been the first converts to Islam and had left their homes and blood ties in Mecca to follow Muhammad to Medina. They believed that since they were Muhammad's first supporters, they had a stronger claim than the Medinans did, and thus Muhammad's successor should be chosen from among their number. After much argument, the

A painting depicts the mosque at Medina which contains Muhammad's tomb. After the prophet died, controversy erupted over who should succeed him.

people of Medina agreed to accept one of the companions, Abu Bakr, as the new leader, or the "representative of the emissary of God." This title in Arabic is *Khalifat rasul Allah*, and it was soon shortened to *Khalifa*, or caliph.

THE RIDDAH WARS

Abu Bakr was immediately faced with the problem of holding together the crumbling Islamic state. Powerful tribes had paid allegiance to Muhammad, but after his death they no longer considered themselves allies of the Muslim community. Religion had always rested lightly upon the Bedouin. They accepted Islam when it was convenient for them, but after Muhammad died, they returned to their old ways and drove away the tax collectors. The Arabic term for "falling away," or secession, is *riddah*. In what became known as the Riddah Wars, Abu Bakr sent an army against these tribes, led by Khalid ibn al-Walid. Abu Bakr insisted that there would be no compromise; he demanded unconditional surrender from the rebels. Khalid, who became known as the "Sword of God" because of his spectacular successes in the Riddah Wars, thoroughly defeated the tribes that had seceded, bringing them back under the authority of Abu Bakr and the young Islamic state.

Despite Abu Bakr's success in the Riddah Wars, his authority was open to challenge. For one thing, rival prophets were a serious problem. Seeing the opportunity for rising to power, some people claimed that they too had received revelations from God. Abu Bakr turned his attention to this threat. The most important and powerful of these threats was the prophet Maslama. Although the Muslims mocked him with the name Musailama, meaning "small or miserable Maslama," he had gained a following even before the death of Muhammad. Maslama joined forces with a Christian woman named Sajah, who also claimed to be a prophet. He married Sajah, and their combined armies numbered in the thousands. Maslama defeated two Muslim armies before Khalid defeated him.

The Riddah Wars had transformed the Arabian Peninsula into an armed camp, with the forces loyal to Abu Bakr fighting various tribes in an effort to force them

CALIPH ABU BAKR'S FIRST ADDRESS

Abu Bakr was chosen as Muhammad's successor, becoming the first caliph. Upon accepting this position, he gave an address to the Muslims. This address, recorded by Muslim chroniclers of the time, and which is reproduced at the Web site anwary-islam.com, set the tone for what people would expect from their caliphs.

I have been given authority over you, and I am not the best of you. If I do well, help me; and if I do wrong, set me right. Sincere regard for truth is loyalty and disregard for truth is treachery. The weak amongst you shall be strong with me until I have secured his rights, if God will; and the strong amongst you shall be weak with me until I have wrested from him the rights of others, if God will. Obey me so long as I obey God and His Messenger [Muhammad]. But if I disobey God and His Messenger, ye owe me no obedience. Arise for your prayer. God have mercy upon you.

back to Islam, to convert those tribes that had never really accepted Islam, or to defeat other tribes whose prophets challenged Islam. Abu Bakr was fortunate in having Khalid ibn al-Walid on his side. Within six months, the brilliant leader brought the tribes of the Arabian Peninsula into submission.

At the end of the Riddah Wars, a political hierarchy of the fledgling Islamic state took shape. At the top were the ruling elite, which included the caliph, Abu Bakr, and his close associates. Next were those who had backed the elite during the Riddah Wars. At the bottom of the hierarchy were those who had refused to acknowledge Abu Bakr's authority and who had been defeated by his armies.

A New Focus

The Riddah Wars were part of a more basic problem that Abu Bakr faced: how to maintain unity among tribes that for untold generations had fought among themselves. While Islam was a unifying force, many of the tribes were not fully committed to Islam. Muhammad himself had acknowledged that the Bedouin were not sincere in their religious beliefs: "The [Bedouin] say 'We have adopted the Faith.' Say [to them] 'Faith ye have not. Rather say: We have become Muslim. For faith has not yet entered your hearts.'"[14] Despite the Riddah Wars, the Bedouin had only grudgingly acknowledged the authority of Abu Bakr, and the cultural heritage of feuding and making war was still strong. Abu Bakr needed to redirect the energies of the Arabian tribes.

To Abu Bakr, expanding the tiny Islamic state he had inherited seemed to be the solution, one that had several advantages. First, sending warriors out on a mission of conquest gave the Arab tribes who had previously fought unceasingly among themselves a new objective. Furthermore, it would bring other Arabic-speaking tribes in the region under control of the Islamic state and spread the religion of Islam. Just as important were the economic advantages: the control of trade, the receipt of tribute from other tribes, and the chance for the Bedouin to share in the wealth of the settled tribes.

The economic advantages were perhaps the most compelling to many of the Bedouin. According to an Arab poet of the time:

> No, not for Paradise didst thou the nomad life forsake;
> Rather, I believe, it was thy yearning after bread and dates. [15]

Abu Bakr energetically pursued the expansion of Islam. Led by remarkable military genius, the Muslim warriors burst out of the Arabian Peninsula, taking the world by surprise. According to Hitti,

> After the death of the Prophet [Muhammad] sterile Arabia seems to have been converted as if by magic into a nursery of heroes the like of whom both in number and quality is hard to find anywhere. The military campaigns of [Khalid ibn al-Walid] and Amr ibn-al-As, which ensued in [Iraq], Persia, Syria and Egypt, are among the most brilliantly executed

in the history of warfare and bear favourable comparison with those of Napoleon, Hannibal or Alexander [the Great].[16]

Abu Bakr died in 634, but the conquest he had set in motion was not to be stopped. On his deathbed Abu Bakr chose Umar, another of Muhammad's closest companions, to succeed him. Umar oversaw the continued expansion of Islam.

THE CONQUEST OF SYRIA

To Abu Bakr and then to Umar, the logical route for expansion of the empire seemed to lie to the north, where Syria, with its important trade center, Damascus, was located. Not only was Syria a rich prize but a relatively easy one. Syria was at the edge of the Byzantine Empire, which was created when the Roman Empire split in two in A.D. 395. The elite city dwellers of Syria had been "Hellenized"—that is, influenced by the Greek culture of the Byzantines. However, Syrians in the countryside had maintained their Arab culture. As a consequence, many of the people of Syria felt more of a kinship with the invading Muslim warriors than with their Byzantine overlords. And for all their Greek ways, the people of the cities had little affection for the Byzantines. For most inhabitants, then—city or rural—transferring loyalty

The lure of Damascus, an important trade center, drove Abu Bakr (left) and his successor Umar (right) to expand the Islamic Empire into Syria.

The Death of Muhammad

Umar, one of Muhammad's closest companions, was the first to see Muhammad on his deathbed. He was so shocked at the thought of the Prophet's death that he reportedly drew his sword and exclaimed, "If anyone says that the Messenger of Allah is dead, I will cut off his head." In the midst of this confusion, Abu Bakr, another of Muhammad's trusted friends and companions, arrived at the bedside where the Prophet lay dead. He reportedly kissed the cheeks of Muhammad and covered his face. Outside, the news of Muhammad's death had reached the people, and they were overcome with grief and confusion. Abu Bakr stepped outside and spoke these famous words of reassurance to the people, as recorded by Muslim chroniclers of the time:

> O people! If anyone among you worshipped Muhammad, let him know that Muhammad is dead. But those who worship Allah, let him know that He lives and will never die.

from the Byzantines to the Arabs was a simple matter.

Another factor that worked in the Muslims' favor was that plagues and war had weakened the Byzantine Empire and its enemy, the Persian Empire. The general prosperity of the lands bordering the Mediterranean Sea had declined.

In 634, Arab armies led by Amr ibn al-As moved toward Syria and Palestine (just south of Syria), where they met stiffer resistance than expected from the Byzantine forces. Meanwhile, Khalid led an army toward the east into Iraq, where he quickly captured parts of the southern region of the Tigris-Euphrates river valley. Khalid next led his army of over five hundred men from Iraq across a brutal, waterless portion of the Syrian desert to reinforce the Arabs in Syria. Khalid's

journey across the desert became legendary. Hitti describes it:

> Water for the troops was carried in bags; but for the horses the paunches of the old camels, later to be slaughtered for food, served as reservoirs. The troops, five to eight hundred in all, rode camels; the few horses to be used at the time of the encounter were led alongside. At one spot Rafi [the guide], with eyes so dazzled by the rays of the sun reflected from the sand that he could not see the expected sign for water, besought the men to look for a box-thorn [bush]. As they dug near it they struck damp sand whence water trickled forth, to the relief of the distressed army.[17]

An Islamic army prepares to go into battle. During the 630s, Arab armies battled Byzantine forces for control of Syria and Palestine.

Within eighteen days, Khalid's army arrived near the Syrian city of Damascus. The army swept down the east side of the Jordan River, and in July 634 joined other Muslim troops to engage the Byzantines at the Battle of Ajnadain.

Once again, Khalid triumphed. The victory opened the way to all of Palestine. Khalid's victories continued, and in September 635, after a six-month siege, the ancient city of Damascus surrendered to the Muslims.

Despite the fall of Damascus, much of Syria was still under Byzantine control. The decisive battle for all of Syria came in August 636. A Byzantine army was encamped in the valley of the Yarmuk River, a tributary of the Jordan River. According to Muslim observers of the time, the day of the battle was windy, with blowing sand and dark skies. The Muslims mounted a terrific onslaught against the Byzantine army, driving them back. Many Byzantines were killed and the panic-stricken survivors fled, leaving the battlefield—and the entire interior of Syria—to the warriors of Allah. On hearing news of the defeat, the Byzantine emperor Heraclius lamented, "Farewell, O Syria, and what an excellent country this is for the enemy!"[18]

Arab armies marched through Syria, whose cities and towns usually surrendered with little resistance. While Khalid and his armies were conquering Syria, another Arab army marched into Palestine, finally capturing Jerusalem in 638. The Christian patriarch of the city insisted that Caliph Umar personally accept the surrender of the city. Historian Wilson Bishai outlines the terms of surrender:

1. The Muslims were to be responsible for the defense of Jerusalem and the protection of its inhabitants.

2. Non-Muslim scriptuaries [Christians and Jews] were to pay *jizya*, "poll tax," to the Muslims, who became their protectors.

3. Christians were guaranteed freedom of worship on condition that their practices should not interfere with Muslim worship.

4. Converts to Islam were to be exempted from paying tax.[19]

THE CONQUEST OF IRAQ

Once the fate of Syria was sealed, Caliph Umar appointed Sa'd ibn Abi Waqqas to lead a ten-thousand-man army to Iraq, which was then part of the Persian Empire. In 637 the Muslim army confronted the Persians at Kadisiya near the Euphrates River in southern Iraq. The Persian commander Rustum sent a message to Sa'd saying, "I understand that poverty and deprivation caused you to come here. We shall give you sufficient food and supplies if you evacuate our land." According to Arab chronicles, the Muslim response was "God has sent to us his Prophet, . . . and we are happy to follow him. He ordered us to conduct a holy war against the adversaries of our religion. . . . We invite you to worship Allah alone and to believe in his Prophet; otherwise the sword will decide matters between you and us."[20]

Once it became clear that there would be no compromise, both sides prepared for battle. According to Muslim historians, the Arab warriors—who called themselves the wolves of the desert—surprised the Persians by attacking in the dark of night. By daybreak, the Persian army had suffered a decisive defeat. The Muslim victory opened the fertile lowlands of Iraq west of the Tigris River. As had happened in Syria, the subject peoples of Iraq welcomed the Arab conquerors, happy to throw off the yoke of their Persian masters.

The following year, Sa'd set his sights on Ctesiphon, the capital city of the Persian Sassanid dynasty. He led his army across the Tigris River, and even though the river was swollen by spring floods, not a single man was lost in the crossing. Arab chroniclers of the time considered the crossing a miracle, a sure sign that Allah was with his army. Once across the river, Arab troops marched toward Ctesiphon. By the time the invaders arrived in the city, the Persian emperor Yazdegerd and his troops had deserted the capital, and the city lay open.

The Arabs established military bases in the south, in the towns of Basra and Al-Kufa, which they later used as the capital of Iraq. As they had done in Syria, Arab tribes moved into the newly conquered areas.

THE DEFEAT OF PERSIA

Once the Arabs had established a stronghold in southern Iraq, their armies crossed into Persia proper, and by 642 the Arabs were at the border of what is now Pakistan. Other Arab armies swept northward in Iraq. The city of Mosul in northern Iraq was captured in 641. Meanwhile, Yazdegerd, the Sassanid emperor, had fled across the Zagros Mountains, along what today is the border between Iraq and Iran. Caliph Umar, fearing that his troops were moving too far too fast, ordered a halt.

During this pause, Yazdegerd mustered an army of about sixty thousand men. Umar now gave permission for the Muslim armies to engage the enemy. Persian and Arab troops met in what is known as the Battle of Nahavand. Persian troops fought desperately, but the Arab armies dealt them a decisive defeat, calling it the "Victory of Victories." Yazdegerd fled with his crown and jewels, and a few of his followers, but one of his own subjects, greedy for the treasure, murdered him while he hid in a poor hut. Yazdegerd's death brought an end to the great Persian Empire, which had flourished for twelve centuries.

The Arab armies continued their drive and by the mid-600s they had captured the Persian province of Khorasan and established their base in the city of Merv. From there they could extend their control over eastern Persia and continue to push eastward. By 700, Arab armies had crossed the Oxus River (known today as the Amu Dar'ya) and swept toward the city of Kabul, in modern-day Afghanistan. They continued eastward into central Asia, reaching as far east as what today is Kazakhstan, taking control of the city of Samarqand and establishing a presence in central Asia. However, it was not until 751, when an Arab army defeated a Chinese army at the Talus River, that the Muslims established undisputed rule in central Asia.

The Bedouin and Civilization

When Arab armies conquered the Persian capital of Ctesiphon in Iraq, it was the richest, most luxurious city these Bedouin desert tribesmen had ever seen. For the first time, they came into contact with the luxuries of the wealthy and privileged. Many of the tribesmen had joined the armies of Allah in the hope of booty. The city of Ctesiphon was rich beyond their dreams.

However, being sons of the desert, the Bedouin did not always know what to make of the riches of civilization, as evidenced by some of the anecdotes passed on by Arab chroniclers of the time. The Bedouin had never seen camphor, which is a white crystalline substance with a distinctive odor (mothballs are made of camphor), and mistaking it for salt, they used it to cook with. Also, gold was not common in Arabia, and Arab soldiers often offered "the yellow" metal in exchange for "the white" (silver), which of course was of much lesser value than gold.

The Bedouin's lack of familiarity with civilization was demonstrated in other ways as well. According to historian Philip Hitti in *History of the Arabs*, when a certain Arabian warrior was chastised for "selling a nobleman's daughter who fell as his share of booty for only 1000 dirhans, his reply was that he 'never thought there was a number above ten hundred.'"

Meanwhile the conquest of the Persian people was not coming as easily as the defeat of its army. Up to this point, Arab warriors had encountered other Semitic peoples like themselves—that is, they shared a generally common culture and language. The Persians, however, were ethnically different. They had been used to their own national identity and to being an imperial power for centuries. Some cities, therefore, offered resistance to the Arab invaders.

The conquest of Persia proved to be one that influenced the conquerors as much as the conquered. In the following centuries, although Arabic became the official language and the language of the elite in Persia, the culture of Persia greatly influenced that of the Islamic Empire. According to Hitti, Persian art, literature, philosophy, and medicine "became the common property of the Arab world and conquered the conquerors. Some of the most brilliant stars in the intellectual firmament of Islam during its first three centuries were Islamized [Persians]."[21]

The military base at Al-Kufa became the capital city of these newly conquered regions of Iraq and Persia. Even though Caliph Umar insisted on keeping a simple way of life, as the Arabs had lived in the desert, the general Sa'd modeled his residence after the royal palace at Ctesiphon. The desert nomads soon became used to the luxury of a rich, settled life. Al-Kufa would eventually grow to an important city, becoming the intellectual and political center of the Arab world in the east.

CONQUEST IN THE WEST

While the caliph's armies were conquering Iraq and Persia, other Muslim troops were moving westward into Egypt, which was under the control of the Byzantine Empire. Egypt represented an attractive target for the expanding Islamic state. The rich soil of the Nile Valley produced the grain to support the Byzantine capital city of Constantinople. Egypt's own grand capital city, Alexandria, was home to the Byzantine navy and the most important port in Egypt.

The Arab military commander Amr ibn al-As led a column of four thousand riders mounted on camels into Egypt in December 639. City after city fell before the invaders. Bewildered Byzantines did not know what to make of these fierce fighters. These Muslim warriors did not fear death, since Islam taught them that

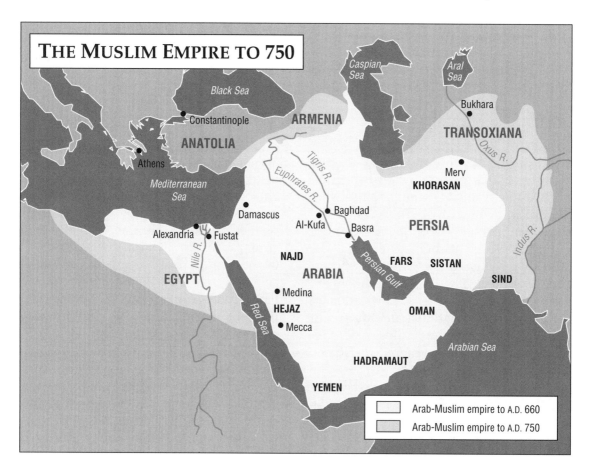

THE MUSLIM EMPIRE TO 750

Arab-Muslim empire to A.D. 660
Arab-Muslim empire to A.D. 750

if they died in battle, they would go immediately to paradise. One Byzantine observer described his adversaries:

> We have witnessed a people to each and every one of whom death is preferable to life, and humility to prominence, and to none of whom this world has the least attraction. They sit not except on the ground, and eat naught but on their knees. Their leader is like unto one of them: the low cannot be distinguished from the high, nor the master from the slave. And when the time of prayer comes none of them absents himself, all wash their extremities and humbly observe their prayer.[22]

Alexandria, however, proved a more difficult problem for the invaders. When Amr reached the city, fresh recruits from Arabia had swelled his army to twenty thousand. But the garrison at Alexandria was fifty thousand strong, backed by the entire Byzantine navy. Furthermore, Alexandria was heavily fortified, and the Arabs had no equipment for breaching the walls. The Byzantine navy controlled access to the city from the sea, and in any case, Amr had no ships. The Arabs controlled the surrounding cities, however. Finally, Cyrus, the leading Christian bishop of Alexandria, decided to strike a deal that allowed him to maintain his own power. In 641 Cyrus concluded a peace treaty with Amr. Under the terms of the treaty, non-Muslims—including Jews—could remain and pay a tax, the Muslims would guarantee the safety of the Christian churches and allow Christians to worship as they pleased, and the Byzantine garrison would evacuate.

Upon the capture of the city, Amr sent a message to Caliph Umar in Medina: "I have captured a city from the description of which I shall refrain. Suffice it to say that I have seized therein 4,000 villas [large homes] with 4,000 baths, 40,000 poll-tax-paying Jews and four hundred places of entertainment for the royalty."[23] Once the Arabs secured Alexandria, they established their provincial capital of Fustat, near present-day Cairo. There they built the first mosque, an Islamic house of worship, in Egypt. The conquest of Egypt was both an economic and military boost for the Arabs. By 644, ships laden with Egyptian goods were unloading at Arab ports. The Arabs also established the first Muslim naval fleet, with Alexandria as the main base. From there the Arabs captured the island of Cyprus, their first maritime victory and the first island in the Islamic Empire.

Throughout the next decade, the Arabs extended their rule along the north coast of Africa to Carthage and Tripoli, subduing the Berber tribes native to the area. By 643, Arabs controlled areas all along the coast of North Africa.

THE ARAB ARMIES AND THE SPREAD OF ISLAM

The stunning military victories of the Arabs surprised the world at the time and continue to amaze historians to this day. At the time it was unthinkable to most observers that small armies of desert tribesmen could defeat imperial forces from the greatest empires on earth. The actual number of Bedouin fighters will probably never be known, since sources of the time exaggerated the numbers, claiming that small numbers of Arab soldiers gloriously won battles against staggering numbers of opposing troops. Almost certainly, the Arabs were outnumbered, but they were generally better equipped and had better leadership than their opponents. Historian F.E. Peters describes the typical Arab fighter:

> The Arab trooper was mounted more often than not on camelback and was protected by a mail helmet and round shield. His offensive weapons were a short, Roman-style sword and a lance. He was [used] to forced marches, short rations and [bad] weather. He could move more

swiftly, maneuver more easily, and had almost exclusive use of the tactical weapon of surprise.[24]

An important factor in the success of the Arab armies was the motivation of their religious beliefs. Muslim historians credit the success of the Islamic warriors to Allah's support. The Arab warriors believed in jihad, or holy war, to spread their faith and that if they died in battle while attempting to spread Islam, they would go immediately to heaven. Consequently, Arab warriors were fierce and fearless in the face of the enemy and in the face of death.

The conquering Arab armies did not completely engulf and lay waste the settled lands. The forces were small and generally well disciplined. Behind the conquering soldiers came large migrations

TERMS OF SURRENDER

When the great warrior hero Khalid ibn al-Walid—the "Sword of God"—captured the city of Damascus in 635, he offered terms of surrender that became a model for the Muslim treatment of other captured cities. In *History of the Arabs,* Philip Hitti includes the terms of surrender offered by Khalid.

> In the name of Allah, the compassionate, the merciful. This is what Khalid ibn-al-Walid would grant to the inhabitants of Damascus if he enters therein: he promises to give them security for their lives, property and churches. Their city wall shall not be demolished, neither shall any Muslim be quartered in their houses. Thereunto we give to them the pact of Allah and the protection of His Prophet, the caliphs and the believers. So long as they pay the poll tax, nothing but good shall befall them.

In this idealized engraving, Muhammad leads an army into jihad, a holy war sanctioned by Allah.

of Arab settlers to claim the land. According to Hourani,

> The interest of the new rulers, however, was to preserve the system of cultivation and therefore of taxation and revenue. Those who had formerly owned the land were largely displaced or else absorbed into the new ruling elite, but the [native] peasantry remained, and soldiers and immigrants were settled on the land or in the new cities.[25]

Thus, within twenty years of Muhammad's death, these warriors of Allah had captured an empire that stretched from central Asia and the fringes of India through the Middle East and along the coast of North Africa to the Atlantic Ocean. All this newly conquered territory was under the administration of the caliph in Medina. Not since the time of Alexander the Great, nearly a thousand years earlier, had so great an empire been under the control of one man.

Chapter

3 Governing an Empire: Umar and the Umayyad Dynasty

The caliph Umar found himself in a difficult position for which he had little preparation. One of the first members of the Quraysh tribe to become a follower of the prophet Muhammad, Umar was from a small desert town, Mecca. Now suddenly he was responsible for an empire that spanned a good part of the known world. The job of ruling such an empire was monumental, but Umar was able to set up effective methods of administration on which his heirs, known to history as the Umayyad dynasty, would build.

DISTRIBUTING THE WEALTH

Two problems Umar faced early on were dividing up the spoils of war and recruiting enough warriors to sustain the expansion. Umar solved the problems by creating a register—in Arabic a *diwan*—that categorized Arab Muslims according to their merit and service to Islam. Those who were relatives of Muhammad, or who had supported him from the beginning, were at the top of the hierarchy. Veterans of the Riddah Wars and soldiers who had joined the Muslim community

(the *ummah*) later on were included in the register but not at the top. The spoils of war, plus the taxes received from the conquered peoples, were placed in a common treasury. Those listed in the *diwan* were paid an annual sum, the amount depending on their status in the register.

The Arabs still maintained the habits of a tribal society, and non-Arab Muslims were still outsiders, although they could become "clients" of an Arab tribesman and receive the protection of his tribe. Non-Arab converts to Islam were not included in the register. In this manner, eventually the register created a kind of aristocracy of Muslim Arabs over non-Arabs.

RELATIONS WITH THE CONQUERED PEOPLES

In addition to determining how to distribute the newly acquired wealth, Umar established the relationship between the conquerors and the conquered peoples. The Arabs considered the Old and New Testament, "the book," as part of sacred scripture, and Jews and Christians were guaranteed protection and religious freedom because they were "people of the book." Nevertheless, all conquered people were required to pay a community land tax, and individuals had to pay a *jizyah*, or a tax for each person counted in the household. If an individual converted to Islam, he was freed from having to pay tribute, or an additional amount over and above taxes. Still, taxes imposed by the Muslims were less than those the people had been paying under the Byzantines or the Persians.

In the early years of the empire, the Arabs did not attempt to occupy the conquered territories or to govern them directly. Instead, they established *amsar*, or military garrisons in conquered regions, such as the garrisons at Basra and Al-Kufa in Iraq, Fustat in Egypt, and Kairouan in Tunisia in North Africa. The military commander of the garrison, known as the emir, collected taxes, supervised the *diwan*, and generally kept order. In general, the conquered people continued to govern themselves, although the emir served as the chief judge of the region. Eventually, as more and more people converted to Islam, the office of emir became more like that of provincial governor, a governor who ruled a province in the name of the central government.

THE DEATH OF UMAR AND THE CALIPHATE OF UTHMAN

Umar's caliphate lasted for ten years. He was considered a man of great piety and justice who lived in the virtuous simplicity of a Bedouin tribal leader. Later Muslim writers revered him as the greatest caliph

in the early years of Islam. His accomplishments earned him a place in history as one of the empire's greatest administrators. Umar established the date of the Hegira (Muhammad's migration from Mecca to Medina) as the beginning of the Muslim era. He oversaw the expansion of the empire and the organization of its government and established the *diwan*. Umar's caliphate ended in 644, when a Persian slave attacked him with a poisoned dagger.

After Umar's death, a small group of respected elders of the Quraysh tribe appointed Uthman ibn Affan as caliph, passing over Muhammad's cousin, Ali. This decision caused tension among the clans of the Quraysh. Ali came from the Hashim clan—the same clan to which Muhammad belonged—while Uthman came from the more powerful Umayyah clan.

Despite the tension, under Uthman, the Arabs completed their conquest of Persia, and continued north, conquering Azerbaijan and parts of Armenia. Arab forces also drove out a Byzantine army that had in the meantime recaptured Alexandria, Egypt.

THE DEATH OF UTHMAN AND CIVIL WAR

The tension between the Umayyads and members of other clans continued to grow. Though Uthman had been an early convert to Islam, others of the Umayyah clan had been fierce opponents of Muhammad. The Umayyads eventually converted to Islam, but those who had

An eighteenth-century painting depicts Uthman ibn Affan, under whose caliphate the Arabs conquered Persia, Azerbaijan, and parts of Armenia.

been Muhammad's earliest companions continued to consider them untrustworthy.

Some of Uthman's own actions contributed to the tension. For example, as was the custom, Uthman placed his relatives in important positions in the empire. Many resented Uthman's actions, especially the Muslims from Medina,

who felt that their influence was being undermined.

The strongest opposition came from Medina from the companions of Muhammad and from Muhammad's widow, A'isha (the first of several wives he had taken following the death of Khadijah). Forces from Egypt joined the opposition and marched to Medina in 656. They stormed Uthman's house, where they found him reading the Koran, and killed him. According to historian Philip Hitti, it was the son of Uthman's friend and predecessor, Abu Bakr, who "broke in and laid the first violent hand upon him. Thus fell the first caliph whose blood was shed by Muslim hands."[26]

After Uthman's death, Ali, of the Hashim clan, was chosen as caliph. At first, most Muslims supported Ali. He was the cousin of Muhammad, husband of Muhammad's favorite daughter, Fatima, and the father of Muhammad's only two surviving male descendants. However, the Umayyads were not willing to give up power so easily. Mu'awiyah, who was Uthman's cousin and governor of Syria, became the head of the Umayyah clan. Now the tribal customs of justice based on revenge came into play. According to tribal custom, it was Mu'awiyah's responsibility to avenge Uthman's death. Mu'awiyah demanded that Ali punish the murderers, but Ali refused to take action. Mu'awiyah then accused Ali of being an accomplice of the murderers.

The murder of Uthman and Ali's refusal to punish the murderers split the Islamic community in half. Arabs from Syria generally supported Mu'awiyah. In Iraq, Arabs in Basra supported Ali. Ali left Medina to settle in Al-Kufa, Iraq, where his supporters were strong.

Civil war followed, and by 657 Ali's forces had the advantage. When it appeared Ali's forces would win, Amr ibn al-As, who commanded Mu'awiyah's forces, attempted a different tactic. He had his soldiers place copies of the Koran on the tips of their lances. This gesture meant that Mu'awiyah was saying the decision should be decided by the Koran rather than by the shedding of Muslim blood. Ali agreed, and one man from each side was appointed to decide the case.

A SINGLE KORAN FOR ALL

One of Uthman's most important accomplishments was his authorization of a standard collection of the suras, or verses of the Koran. From the time of Muhammad's revelations, "readers" had memorized and recited the suras. Parts of the Koran were written down, and by the time of Uthman's caliphate, various collections of the Koran existed. Uthman appointed a commission headed by one of Muhammad's secretaries to compile a single authoritative version of the Koran. This version was distributed to major centers of the empire, and copies of other versions were ordered to be destroyed. This caused resentment among many Muslims, who saw this as the Umayyah clan attempting to gain total control of Islam.

The two judges decided that neither Ali nor Mu'awiyah should be caliph and that a third party should be appointed. Ali was criticized by his own followers, who said that he was already caliph and should punish Mu'awiyah, not negotiate with him. Finally, in 661 as Ali was on his way to prayers at the mosque in Al-Kufa, he was assassinated by some of his own followers who had turned against him. Ali was buried near Al-Kufa in An Najaf, which has become one of Islam's most important pilgrimage centers.

The death of Ali permanently split the Muslim community. With Ali gone, Mu'awiyah became caliph. Most Muslims accepted him, although reluctantly. They called themselves Sunnis ("followers of the sunna" or the "way of the Prophet"). Ali's supporters, who refused to accept Mu'awiyah, became known as Shia or Shiites, followers of Ali. They believed that Ali was the true successor of Muhammad. Ali was soon considered the saint of the Shia. Although he had not proven a great leader, he possessed the traits of the ideal Arab, as Hitti describes: "Valiant in battle, wise in counsel, eloquent in speech, true to his friends, [generous] to his foes, he became both the 'model' of Muslim nobility and chivalry and the Solomon [the biblical king noted for his wisdom] of Arabic tradition."[27]

MU'AWIYAH, THE FIRST UMAYYAD CALIPH

Never again would Muslims be unanimous in their choice of leader. Still, for the time being the real power lay with the Sunni Umayyads. Mu'awiyah's caliphate (661–680) marked the beginning of a new era in political leadership, one in which the caliph's connection to Muhammad was of paramount importance. The first four caliphs—Abu Bakr, Umar, Uthman, and Ali—were remembered as the orthodox caliphs, or as the majority of Muslims called them, the Rashidun, or "rightly guided." According to Hitti, the era of the orthodox caliphs

> was a period in which the lustre of the Prophet's life had not ceased to shed its light and influence over the thoughts and acts of the caliphs. All four were close associates and relatives of the Prophet. They lived in [Medina], the scene of his last ministry, with the exception of the last, Ali, who chose al-Kufah in [Iraq] for his capital.[28]

One of Mu'awiyah's first actions as caliph was to establish his capital in Damascus, Syria, a move that served to put distance between the new caliph and his potential rivals. Many of Ali's supporters were in Medina, while Damascus was closer to the Arab tribes of Syria who supported the Umayyads. In addition, Damascus, unlike Medina, was in a fertile region that could produce enough food to support a royal court, a government, and an army. This made the city virtually self-sufficient.

Mu'awiyah is remembered as a patient ruler, known for his willingness to use force only as a last resort. In his own words, "I apply not my sword where my lash suffices, nor my lash where my tongue is enough. And even if there be one hair binding me to my fellowmen, I

The fourth caliph Ali was assassinated by some of his followers on his way to a mosque. This illustration depicts Muslims at prayer inside a mosque.

do not let it break: when they pull I loosen, and if they loosen I pull."[29] However, not all his subjects considered Mu'awiyah a great leader. Many Muslims of the time were offended that Mu'awiyah acted like a temporal ruler, not a spiritual leader and representative of Muhammad. Indeed, Mu'awiyah and the later Umayyads focused on organizing the empire, which would cause many to oppose them. These opponents were against the secularization, or focus on worldly affairs, that Umayyads represented.

THE MARTYRDOM OF HUSAYN

Islam had been splintered into Sunni and Shiite sects when Mu'awiyah was appointed caliph over Ali. That split widened when Mu'awiyah died in 680 and his son Yazid became caliph. The Shia believed that Husayn, the grandson of Muhammad, should be next in line for the caliphate, and they refused to acknowledge Yazid as the legitimate caliph. Yazid ordered the suppression of the rebellion, while the Shia in Al-Kufa persuaded Husayn to make a claim on the caliphate. Husayn, then living in Mecca, gathered a group of seventy followers, including women and children, and marched toward Al-Kufa. His group was halted at the town of Karbala by an army of four thousand led by one of Yazid's generals. What happened there, on October 20, 680, became one of the most important events in the Shiite sect of Islam. When Husayn refused to turn back, the troops attacked the group. In the bloody massacre, Husayn died while holding his infant son in his arms. The blood of Husayn, even more than that of his father, Ali, was the seed of the Shiite sect. The Shiites became even more fervent enemies of the Umayyad caliphs.

Yazid died less than three years after the Battle of Karbala, and his son, Mu'awiyah II, died that same year (683). A period of instability followed, with rebellious factions within the Umayyads attempting to take over. Power was finally taken by the senior member of the Umayyah clan, Marwan I. Marwan sent armies against the rebels, but had barely begun the task of reestablishing his power when he too died. In 685 the caliphate finally settled on Marwan's son, Abd al-Malik.

EXPANSION UNDER THE UMAYYAD CALIPHATE

The Umayyads continued to expand their empire, which eventually grew so large that further expansion was not practical. They established their first important base in North Africa at Kairouan, in what is now Tunisia. They continued their westward march along Africa's coast until they reached Morocco on the

THE LEGENDS OF HUSAYN

Husayn, the grandson of Muhammad who was killed at the battle of Karbala, achieved the status of holy martyr in the eyes of Shiite Muslims. Over the centuries, legends emerged about Husayn that supposedly confirmed that he was blessed by Allah as a holy martyr.

One legend states that on the day of Husayn's birth, Allah sent the angel Gabriel to earth to congratulate Muhammad on the birth of his grandson. Descending from heaven, Gabriel passed over an island where the angel Futrus had been banished and deprived of his wings because he had displeased Allah. Futrus called out to Gabriel, asking where he was going. When Gabriel told him his mission, Futrus asked Gabriel to carry him along so that he could ask Muhammad to intercede for him. Gabriel complied, and when Futrus presented his case to Muhammad, Muhammad instructed Futrus to touch the body of the newborn Husayn. Futrus did this, and his wings were immediately restored, and he returned to his place in heaven.

According to another legend, when Husayn was killed at the battle of Karbala and his severed head was placed on the point of a lance, it began to speak. His lips glorified God, saying, "Allahu Akbar" [God is great]. "All glory be to Allah Who is the greatest."

Atlantic coast at the end of the seventh century. From there a combined army of Arabs and Berber tribesmen—who had converted to Islam—began a swift conquest of Spain in 711. Their leader, Tariq ibn Ziyad, landed near the great rock that now bears his name: Jabal of Tariq ("Mount of Gibraltar"). The defending army consisting of twenty-five thousand Visigoth warriors was soundly defeated by the Muslim force. By 713 the Muslims controlled Spain, which they named al-Andalus, or in English, Andalusia.

The Muslims reached their limits in Europe in 732 when they crossed the Pyrenees and marched into southern France. Near the city of Tours, the army of Frankish leader Charles Martel engaged the Muslims, killing their leader Abd ar-Rahman and defeating their cavalry. The Muslim defeat at the Battle of Tours (sometimes called the Battle of Poitiers) is considered by Europeans to be a decisive victory, since it stopped the spread of Islam in Europe. The Muslims, however, regarded it as a minor battle. Their control of their empire was already stretched thin. They were content to remain in the sunny plains of southern Spain, a climate more to their liking than the cold of northern Europe.

Although the Muslims did not move any farther into Europe, in the east, Arab armies marched deep into Persia, beyond the region of Khorasan, and into northwestern India. They continued on into central Asia, where they reached the edge of the Tang Empire of China.

Arab forces took control of eastern Mediterranean sea routes, which allowed them to control trade. Meanwhile, Arab armies assaulted the ancient city of Constantinople, capital of the Byzantine Empire, although that attack failed.

THE RULE OF THE UMAYYAD CALIPHATE

The early Umayyad caliphs reflected their desert heritage. Unlike the first four caliphs following Muhammad, they did not consider themselves first and foremost as religious leaders. They ruled in the manner of their Bedouin ancestors, as desert chieftains. The cosmopolitan city of Damascus, with its Byzantine influences, was foreign to them. The Bedouin wife of one of the early caliphs expressed her longing for her life in the desert: "The tent unprotected against gusts of strong winds is dearer to me than this palace. The rough woollen gown I wore was far more precious to me than these fine dresses. I relished eating a crumb of dry bread in a corner of my dwelling better than these fresh loaves of white bread."[30]

Over time, however, the Umayyads became accustomed to the pleasures of Byzantine civilization. They adapted the old Byzantine bureaucracy to help administer their empire, and gradually they developed a way of life less like desert chieftains and more like other rulers of the Near East. They established a palace court and royal bodyguards. They had an entourage of attendants to care for their every personal need. And they established ceremonies and customs like those of a Byzantine emperor.

The Byzantine bureaucracy was well suited to the expanding empire and provided the model for a more efficient

A mosaic depicts the sixth-century Byzantine emperor Justinian and his court. During the eighth century, the Umayyads modeled their bureaucracy after that of the Byzantines.

government. First, the army was made a professional organization with paid soldiers, displacing the old units bound together by tribal loyalties.

In the provinces of Iraq, the great canal between the Tigris and Euphrates rivers was restored, and new canals were built. New lands were drained and cultivated, adding to the agricultural prosperity of the region.

In the financial administration of the empire, the methods and people that had served the previous rulers were taken over by the new Arab rulers. While the bureaucrats of the old empires remained the same, the Arabs changed the official language of administration to Arabic. Civil servants who spoke Arabic

continued to serve in the government, and many converted to Islam, especially in Syria. The acceptance of Islam also implied the acceptance of Arabic as the language of revelation. Through its use in government, and through Islam, Arabic was becoming the common language of the empire.

The new Arab rulers followed the customs of the old regime in the Syrian countryside as well, as Hourani describes:

They seem carefully to have maintained the systems of irrigation and cultivation which they found there, and the palaces and houses they built to serve as centres of economic control as well as hospitality were arranged and decorated in the style of the rulers they had replaced, with audience-halls and baths, mosaic floors, sculptured doorways and ceilings.[31]

Even though the Arabs adopted many of the customs of the previous rulers, they were not completely swallowed up in the culture of those they had conquered. Indeed, the Arabs brought something that set them apart from the old Byzantine and Persian cultures: their belief in the teachings of the prophet Muhammad and the Arabic language in which those teachings were expressed.

Islam's stamp was apparent throughout the conquered lands. For example, the Arabs introduced new coinage that was imprinted not with images of a human leader but with Arabic script proclaiming the teachings of Muhammad. More important, and a sign of the permanence of the new empire, was the construction of monumental buildings. Many existing buildings were taken over as mosques.

The first great building was the Dome of the Rock in Jerusalem, commissioned by Caliph Malik. The Dome of the Rock was created not as a mosque but as a sacred shrine, or *haram.* Later, great mosques were built in a number of important cities. The buildings were designed with an open courtyard and a covered space in which long lines of worshippers could

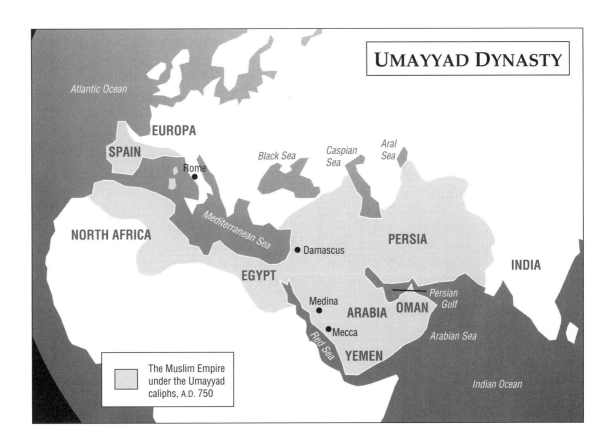

pray facing in the direction of Mecca. A minaret, or tall tower, was either attached to or near the mosque, from which a muezzin, or Muslim crier, could call the faithful to prayer.

Caliph al-Walid (705–715) was the greatest builder of the Umayyad caliphs. He enlarged and improved the mosque of Mecca and rebuilt the mosque in Medina. He built schools and places of worship and was the first medieval ruler to build hospitals for the chronically sick, practices that were only later imitated by Europeans.

Al-Walid's greatest accomplishment was the building of the Great Mosque in Damascus. The mosque was constructed on the site of what had been an early Greek temple and which was later a Christian church. The walls were covered with magnificent mosaics depicting scenes of paradise as described in the Koran. Construction of magnificent structures such as this was a sign to the world that the Arabs were there to stay.

The new mosques also signaled the growth of a community of believers. Islam was no longer simply the faith of the ruling class. Throughout the growing empire, subject peoples converted to Islam for a variety of reasons. Those who worked for the new rulers might convert to gain personal advantage, such as appointment to more important positions in the government that were reserved for Muslims. Conversion to Islam also meant that the special taxes levied on non-Muslims could be avoided.

The straightforward nature of Islam was part of its appeal. The Christian church at the time was bedeviled by controversies about the nature of God, and some Christians may have been attracted to the simplicity of the Muslim belief about the unity of the one God. Moreover, conversion to Islam did not involve any elaborate rituals. The simple affirmation that "there is no God but God and Muhammad is His Prophet" was all that was needed.

THE FALL OF THE UMAYYAD CALIPHATE

Yet the growth in the community of Muslims did not greatly benefit the Umayyad caliphate, with its capital in Syria. The cities of Syria were already well established. It was the eastern portion of the empire, including Iraq, that was the fastest growing. Immigrants from the Arabian Peninsula and from Persia flooded into Iraq to populate the countryside and the newly established cities that had begun as Arab military outposts. The same thing was happening in the region of Khorasan in Persia, at the edge of the Arab expansion into central Asia, where there were large garrisons. The land of Khorasan was fertile and attracted Arab settlers; members of the old Persian ruling class of the region turned their skills to administering the new empire.

Still, the expansion of the empire actually strengthened one aspect of Arab culture. As Arab tribesmen—who had previously been spread out across the Arabian steppe—settled down in one region or city, their tribal ties strengthened and tribal chiefs grew more powerful. Often the interests of these tribes and their leaders were at odds with those of the Umayyad rulers in Damascus.

Caliph al-Walid built the Great Mosque in Damascus during the early eighth century.

At the same time, expansion bred ethnic tension. While many people converted to Islam, they did not have the same status or enjoy the same privileges as Arab Muslims. As a result, resentment among the non-Arab converts began to grow, especially among the Persians, who had been used to occupying a privileged position before the fall of the Sassanid dynasty.

Gradually the interests of the Arabs in the eastern provinces—many of whom were Shia—combined with the interests of non-Arab Muslims, especially Persians, to spark a revolution. The Shia had never forgiven the Umayyads for the martyrdom of Husayn and for taking the caliphate from Ali, whom they considered as having had the only legitimate claim. Leading the revolutionary movement were the descendants of al-'Abbas, the uncle of the prophet Muhammad. The Abbasids, as these descendants are known, exploited the dissatisfaction of the Shia, pointing out the decadence of the pleasure-loving Umayyads as a contrast to their own piety.

In June 747 the revolt began. The Persians from Khorasan, the Shia, and the Abbasids went to war under a black banner, which had originally been the emblem of Muhammad himself. The revolutionaries took Merv, the capital of Khorasan. Marwan, the caliph in Damascus, had problems at home with other insurgents and was unable to send an army to defend his eastern provinces.

Meanwhile, Abu al-Abbas, the leader of the Abbasids, was in Al-Kufa, Iraq, when the insurgents captured the city in 749. On October 30, 749, in the chief mosque in Al-Kufa, Abu al-Abbas was declared caliph. Abu al-Abbas was also known by the name as-Saffah ("blood shedder"), a title that later events proved he well deserved. In January 750, Marwan led an army of twelve thousand men to meet the Abbasid forces led by Abdullah, the uncle of the new caliph. Marwan's army was soundly defeated. Marwan fled, and the Abbasid army marched westward, taking towns one after another until it reached Damascus, which it captured in a few days. Marwan had fled to Egypt, where he was hunted down and killed. His head was sent to Abu al-Abbas.

The Abbasids followed the execution of Marwan with a campaign of extermination of all members of the Umayyah clan. General Abdullah invited an unsuspecting group of eighty Umayyads to a banquet, where, according to Hitti, "in the course of the feast [Abdullah] had them all cut down. After spreading leathern covers over the

THE REMARKABLE SUKAYNAH

In early Islam under the Umayyads, women enjoyed much more freedom than they did under the later caliphs. One of the most remarkable women of this period was Sukaynah, daughter of the martyred Husayn and granddaughter of Ali. Noted for her charm, good taste, wit, and humor, she was a hostess of rare talent who attracted the most fashionable people of the city to her gatherings.

She enjoyed jests and hoaxes, and in one example of rather crude humor, to amuse her guests she had a Persian sheikh sit on a basket of eggs and cluck like a hen.

Sukaynah was so captivating that she had a numerous succession of husbands, one of whom was the brother of the caliph Umar II. In her marriages, she insisted on complete freedom of action.

dead and dying he and his lieutenants continued their [feast] to the accompaniment of human groans."[32]

The extermination continued, with Abbasid agents sent throughout the empire to hunt down members of the Umayyad family. One important member of the Umayyad family escaped, however. The young Abd ar-Rahman managed to reach Spain safely, where he eventually established an offshoot of the Umayyad dynasty. With the destruction of the Umayyads, the stage was set for a new era of the Islamic Empire, the era of the lavish and brilliant Abbasid caliphate.

4 The Abbasid Caliphate

Under the direction of the prophet Muhammad and the early caliphs, the religion of Islam became the foundation of a nation of believers. The widespread conquests under the Umayyads turned that nation into a world power. The dynasty that followed, built on the earlier gains, created a strong and lasting empire.

A New Caliphate, a New Capital

The Abbasids had won their throne in A.D. 750 mainly by assembling a coalition of those who opposed the Umayyads. Now it was up to the Abbasid caliphs to consolidate and concentrate their power. That process proved a bloody one. First, Abu al-Abbas eliminated those who had helped him achieve power but who might also someday oppose him. For example, when some who had previously supported Abu al-Abbas refused to obey his newly appointed governors, the caliph made an example of them. In the city of Mosul, Iraq, he requested the inhabitants to gather in the courtyard of a mosque so that he could hear their complaints, promising them security. When about ten thousand people gathered, Abu al-Abbas sent in his troops, who surrounded and slaughtered the people. The caliph's bloody methods soon silenced any opposition.

Following Abu al-Abbas's death in 754, his successor, al-Mansur, further consolidated Abbasid power. He established a new ruling elite, many of whom were Persians who had served the previous rulers. Under al-Mansur the office of the vizier, a high-ranking official who served as adviser and administrator, was established.

With the rise of the Abbasids, the center of power of the Islamic Empire shifted to the east. Abbasid allies were mainly in Iraq and eastward into Khorasan and central Asia. Abu al-Abbas kept his capital at Al-Kufa. But al-Mansur decided on a new site for the capital of Islam: the city of Baghdad in Iraq.

A Diverse Society

Under the Umayyad caliphate, while power lay in Damascus, the Arabs had maintained supremacy within the empire, even though many non-Arabs were converting to Islam. Now, with the center of the empire in Baghdad, the Islamic Empire became more culturally diverse.

Under the Abbasids, Persians gained influence in the Islamic Empire. The viziers were Persian, and most of the Abbasids' soldiers were recruited from the Persian province of Khorasan. Yet the empire was home to many other cultures. In addition to Arabs and Persians, Turks and other peoples from central Asia were also part of the Islamic Empire.

Despite its diversity of peoples, however, by the ninth or tenth century the empire had developed a common Islamic culture that bound its people together. A traveler from elsewhere could tell by the language, architecture, and customs of the people whether he or she was in the Islamic world.

THE BONDS OF EMPIRE

Until the time of the Abbasids, however, Islam remained a minority faith in the empire. Scholars estimate that at the end

THE VICTORY OF ABU AL-ABBAS

In 750 the last Umayyad caliph was killed and Abu al-Abbas was proclaimed the new caliph, the first of the Abbasid caliphs. In Hourani's *A History of the Arab Peoples*, Arab historian al-Tabari (839–923) describes how Dawud, brother of Abu al-Abbas, announced the victory from the steps of the mosque in Al-Kufa.

> Praise be to God, with gratitude, gratitude, and yet more gratitude! Praise to him who has caused our enemies to perish and brought to us our inheritance from Muhammad our Prophet, God's blessing and peace be upon him! O ye people, now are the dark nights of the world put to flight, its covering lifted, now light breaks in the earth and the heavens, and the sun rises from the springs of day while the moon ascends from its appointed place. He who fashioned the bow takes it up, and the arrow returns to him who shot it. Right has come back to where it originated, among the people of the house of your Prophet, people of compassion and mercy for you and sympathy toward you. . . . God has let you behold what you were awaiting and looking forward to. He has made manifest among you a caliph of the clan of Hashim, brightening thereby your faces and making you to prevail over the army of Syria, and transferring the sovereignty and the glory of Islam to you. . . . Has any successor to God's messenger ascended this your *minbar* save the Commander of the Faithful 'Ali ibn Abi Talib and the Commander of the Faithful 'Abd Allah ibn Muhammad?—and he gestured with his hand toward Abu'l-'Abbas.

of the Umayyad caliphate only about 10 percent of the population of Syria, Egypt, Iraq, and Persia were Muslim (although in the Arabian Peninsula the percentage was much greater). Under the Umayyads, the converts to Islam were generally prisoners of war and officials of conquered provinces who stayed on to serve the new rulers. These converts usually lived in or near large cities. However, during the Abbasid caliphate, many more people converted to Islam, and the majority of the empire's subjects became Muslim.

Belief in the oneness of God and the message of the prophet Muhammad gave people of all ethnicities a common bond. Every day—five times a day—people from Spain in the west to Turkmenistan in the east faced the Arabian city of Mecca, spread their prayer rugs, and bowed in prayer. Across the empire, in all the great cities, the devout filled mosques every Friday to participate in common prayer. They performed the same gestures and repeated the same words from the Koran. The faithful honored the same practices required of Muslims, such as praying daily, fasting during Ramadan, and giving *zakat*, or alms, to the poor. People were aware of belonging to a community of believers—the *ummah*. Their shared beliefs linked them to one another while distinguishing them from people who practiced other religions.

Every year thousands of people traveled to Mecca to perform the ritual pilgrimage, the hajj, which Islam requires a believer to do once in a lifetime. Pilgrims came from every corner of the empire, from Cordoba in Spain to the ancient city of Samarqand in Uzbekistan

A painting depicts a congregation of Muslims praying at a mosque in Mecca. Islam requires all Muslims to make the pilgrimage to Mecca at least once before they die.

in the easternmost reaches of the empire. Many of these pilgrims—Turks, Berbers, Arabs, Persians—who converged on Mecca spoke the common language of Islam and the Koran, Arabic. Imperial officials, civil servants, teachers, and scholars all spoke Arabic. As a result, an official from Toledo, Spain, and a scholar from Kabul, Afghanistan, who met in Mecca could converse together. Sharing a language gave the Islamic Empire an Arabic flavor regardless of which ethnic group was gaining influence. Al-Biruni, an eleventh-century writer of Persian origin, notes the persistence of the empire's Arab identity: "How often have the tribes of subjects congregated together in order to impart a non-Arab character to the State! But they could not succeed in their aim."[33]

That Arabic character—and Islam itself—continued to broaden its influence. The Umayyads had extended the reach of Islam through their military might. Under the Abbasids, Islam was spread through trade and commerce.

THE ECONOMIC BASIS OF THE EMPIRE

Besides spreading Islam, trade contributed greatly to prosperity in the Islamic Empire. In the conquered countries, a new class of Arab landholders arose. As these landholders accumulated money, they invested it in new agricultural techniques. New crops were introduced, mainly from the east, including rice, cotton, watermelons, oranges, lemons, and sugarcane. These crops required improved irrigation and cultivation techniques. Irrigation systems that had fallen into disrepair were restored or new ones were built. Again the movement of new techniques in agriculture moved from east to west: The waterwheel was introduced into Spain from Syria, and the use of underground canals was introduced from Persia. These improvements led to an agricultural surplus, helping to feed ever-larger urban populations and increase the overall prosperity of the empire.

The empire was economically powerful in part because of its sheer size, but also because of its location between the Mediterranean Sea and the Indian Ocean—the two great waterways that had always provided ancient civilizations with a means of moving goods. The growing cities of the empire created a large new market for luxury items and for the new and exotic trade goods carried by oceangoing vessels. The free travel between the Mediterranean and the Indian Ocean eased the movement of goods (and also of pilgrims, scholars, craftsmen, and armies, and their ideas and techniques). Historian Albert Hourani describes the thriving trade created in the empire:

> Pepper and other spices, precious stones, fine cloth and porcelain came from India and China, furs from the northern countries; coral, ivory and textiles were sent in return. The Middle Eastern cities were not only consumers but also producers of manufactured goods for export as well as their own use. Some of the production was on a large scale—armaments of war produced in state arsenals, fine textiles for the palace,

Merchants in Baghdad display their wares at a bazaar. Due to its strategic location, the Iraqi city became the center of the Islamic Empire's trade network.

sugar refineries and paper mills—but most took place in small workshops for textiles or metalwork.[34]

Baghdad was the center of this grand network of trade. Its location at the hub of waterways and overland routes made it the meeting place for traders from around the empire. Arab merchant ships set sail down the Tigris River to Basra, where the river flows into the Persian Gulf and beyond to the Indian Ocean and to ports in the east. Camel caravans traveled overland to and from Asia to the east, Africa to the south, and Damascus, Cairo, and Mediterranean ports in the

west. Arab traders sailed the Mediterranean along the African coast and then north to Spain, bringing the riches of the East and Middle East to Europe and returning with Spanish silk, olive oil, and the world-renowned swords and knives forged of steel in the workshops of Toledo.

Along with goods, Muslim traders brought their religion and the Arabic language to remote locales. In East Africa, Muslim traders bought gold, cloves, ivory, and slaves from Africans, who received porcelain, cloth, and iron in exchange. Africans adopted the religion of Islam, and the interaction of the Arab and

African traders affected local African languages as well. The result was a new language, Swahili, which spread through much of East Africa.

Muslim traders traveled the Sahara Desert to reach the coast of West Africa, bringing with them salt, which they exchanged for the gold of the African nation of Ghana. Influenced by their trading partners, many West Africans likewise adopted Islam.

CURRENCY AND A BANKING SYSTEM

The access the Abbasids had to large quantities of precious metals, especially gold from Africa, made it possible for them to mint their own coins. This eased the further development of commerce, since goods could be traded for money rather than bartered for bulky, perishable goods such as grain or livestock.

Along with the monetary system came a banking system and a system of credit. Wealthy merchants would act as bankers, taking deposits and making loans. Letters of credit, or checks, could be issued to clients in distant places, ushering in the world's first checking system.

Muslim traders also developed the concept of business partnerships, by which a group of individuals would invest in a venture, such as importing a caravan load of goods from distant places. When the goods were sold, they would

THE ART AND COMMERCE OF TEXTILES

The manufacture of commercial textiles became a fine art under the Abbasids and became one of the empire's most important industries. Weavers were noted for the production of fine tapestries and silk, cotton and woolen fabrics, satin, and brocade. The city of Mosul in northern Iraq produced a fine cotton cloth known today as muslin, after the city of its origin. From Persia came a silken cloth they called *taftah*, which the Europeans called taffeta.

Persia and Iraq were especially noted for their production of beautiful rugs with ornate designs. A rug made especially for the mother of a caliph had figures of birds woven with gold thread. The bird's eyes were made of rubies and other precious stones. High-quality, ornately patterned rugs are still known today as "Persian" rugs.

One particular type of striped fabric made by the Arab weavers in Spain was known as *tabi*. The fabric became popular in European countries, and the name of the fabric survives to this day in the word *tabby*, a name given to striped or marked cats.

share the profits and the losses in proportion to the amount that each had originally invested.

THE ABBASID STATE

This diverse empire with its far-flung trading networks came under the authority of one man—the caliph. From him, all power flowed, at least in theory. Unlike the Umayyad caliphs, Abbasid caliphs emphasized the religious nature and dignity of their office. The caliphs were treated as semidivine rulers and claimed that they held office by "divine right"—in other words, that God had ordained their right to rule. One of the official titles held by later Abbasid caliphs was "Shadow of God on Earth."

Succession to the caliphate was hereditary, with the caliph appointing his son or other family member as his successor. The caliph also appointed a grand vizier, who had authority over civil matters. The vizier, whose office was a part of the Persians' governing practice, could be extremely powerful, depending on the wishes of the caliph. It was customary for the vizier to confiscate, or take over, the property of any provincial governor who fell out of favor and was removed from his position. This practice became so common at the central government level, as well as in the provinces, that a bureau of confiscation was established as a regular government bureau.

That authority could be far reaching. While some caliphs limited the power of their viziers, others gave their viziers complete authority while they pursued other, more pleasurable interests. For example, Caliph an-Nasir (1180–1225) in appointing his vizier made it clear that this representative's authority came from God:

> Muhammad ibn-Barz al-Qummi is our representative throughout the land and amongst our subjects. Therefore he who obeys him obeys us; and he who obeys us obeys God, and God shall cause him who obeys Him to enter Paradise. As for one who, on the other hand, disobeys our vizier, he disobeys us; and he who disobeys us disobeys God, and God shall cause him who disobeys Him to enter hell-fire.[35]

In addition to choosing his vizier, the caliph assigned a general to take charge of military matters and a judge to have authority over legal matters. The caliph, however, remained the final authority in all matters.

As a semidivine person, the caliph separated himself from his subjects. He normally remained concealed from all but his most intimate servants and advisers behind an intricately carved screen or embroidered curtain. His personal retinue included a chamberlain who was responsible for personally escorting visiting dignitaries into the caliph's presence. This practice meant that the chamberlain could have extraordinary influence by controlling who was allowed to see the caliph.

Abbasid caliphs borrowed other elements from the Persian rule. The court executioner stood ready to behead any visitor to the court who offended the caliph. The court astrologer predicted the future and gave advice based on the

An Abbasid caliph receives visitors. The Abbasid caliphs were treated as semidivine, and they claimed that God had granted them the right to rule.

The caliph watches as the court executioner beheads a criminal. The Abbasids borrowed this method of punishment from the Persians.

positions of heavenly bodies. The Abbasids also introduced the Persian practice of torture of prisoners for the first time in Arab history, building underground torture chambers.

While the government under the Abbasids became more complex, it also became more orderly, especially in the areas of taxes and the judicial system. The Bureau of Taxes was headed by a "master of taxes," an important and powerful office in the government. The most important responsibility of the master of taxes was collection of the *zakat*, or tax for the poor,

which every Muslim was obligated by the Koran to pay. The *zakat* was collected on cultivated land, herd animals, commercial goods, and gold and silver. The *zakat* was distributed to help the Muslim poor, orphans, strangers, slaves, and volunteers for holy wars.

The master of taxes also collected taxes paid by non-Muslims. Individual non-Muslim subjects paid a personal tax, while conquered former enemies paid tribute. In addition, goods owned by non-Muslims or imported into the Islamic Empire by non-Muslims were taxed. Especially during the early years of the Abbasid caliphate, the taxes collected allowed the caliph to live in grand luxury.

Another important agency within the government was the police. The head of the police was a high official who also acted as the head of the royal bodyguards. Each large city had a chief of police, whose job, according to Hitti, was

> to see that proper weights and measures were used in trade, that legitimate debts were paid (although he had no judicial power), that approved morals were maintained and that acts forbidden by law, such as gambling, usury [excessive interest charged for loans] and public sale of wine were not committed.[36]

The chief of police was also responsible for enforcing standards of morality in relations between men and women, which, Hitti notes, included punishing men "who dyed their grey beards black with a view to gaining the favour of the ladies."[37]

Another important bureau was the postal department. A postal service had first been instituted under the Umayyads, and this extended throughout the empire. The postal service was primarily for the use of government officials, although individuals could use it in a limited way. The capital of each province had a post office. Routes connected the post offices in important cities to the imperial capital. Along the routes were relay stations, and mail was carried by a series of relays. In Persia mail and dispatches were carried by mules and horses and by camels in Syria and Arabia. Carrier pigeons, birds with a strong homing instinct, were also used to carry letters. The headquarters in Baghdad had records of all the routes, relay stations, and distances between each.

The postal director also acted as the chief of the empire's spy system. Provincial postmasters were responsible for reporting to the postal director in the capital on the behavior of other provincial officials. In this way, the caliph was able to keep an eye on officials in his empire.

Because of the size of the empire, it was impossible for the caliph to maintain a strong central control, even with his network of spies. Although in theory the local governors served at the pleasure of the vizier, because they had the authority to confiscate property, they (just as the vizier himself did) wielded nearly absolute power in their provinces. Indeed, the office of governor eventually became hereditary.

THE MILITARY UNDER THE ABBASIDS

The royal bodyguard overseen by the chief of police was the nucleus of a larger professional army. Soldiers were well paid, with the foot soldiers receiving about half the pay that the cavalry received. At the height of the empire's power, the army numbered about 125,000 men.

The infantry was armed with swords, spears, and shields. The army included archers as well as cavalrymen, who carried long lances and battle-axes and wore helmets. In addition, there were engineers who supervised the siege machines, such as catapults and battering rams. The army was equipped with field hospitals and ambulances in the form of camels that carried litters.

During the first century of the Abbasid caliphate, the army was used to support the caliph, to suppress revolts, and to wage war against the Byzantine Empire. Their large numbers, the skill in military tactics, and the swiftness with which they could move made them formidable foes. The Byzantine emperor Constantine Porphyrogenitus (913–959) wrote of his impression of the Arab warriors: "They are powerful and warlike, so that if only a thousand of them occupy a

A thirteenth-century illustration depicts soldiers on camels patrolling the streets of Baghdad. The Abbasid cavalry also used camels instead of horses.

CALIPH HARUN AND THE BYZANTINES

Harun ar-Rashid is one of the most well remembered Abbasids, primarily because many of the tales from *The Thousand and One Nights* take place in Baghdad under his rule. Harun is not so well remembered for his conflicts with the Byzantines, however. During a war with the Byzantines, he compelled the Empress Irene to pay him tribute. When a new Byzantine emperor, Nicephorus I, took the throne, he reversed Irene's agreement, sending the following message to Harun (quoted in Bishai's *Islamic History of the Middle East*):

> From Nicephorus, king of the Romans, to Harun, king of the Arabs. The queen who preceded me . . . carried to you from her wealth that which you should have doubled and carried to her. However, this was due to women's weakness and foolishness. Therefore, when you read my message, return the wealth which you have received and save yourself the consequences. Otherwise, the sword will determine matters between us and you.

To which Harun replied:

> In the name of the Lord, the merciful, the compassionate, From Harun, the Commander of the Faithful, to Nicephorus, the dog of the Romans. I read your message, Oh son of a pagan mother. My reply to you will be seen rather than heard.

Harun and the Byzantines resumed war, and once again Harun won, forcing the Byzantines to pay him tribute.

camp it is impossible to dislodge them. They do not ride horses, but camels."[38]

Under later caliphs, the military might of the Abbasids declined with the introduction of foreign troops. Causing further decline was the practice of assigning provinces to military commanders, who paid their troops from the local funds collected in the province rather than paying them from the imperial treasury. This practice encouraged short-term exploitation of the land and the people who farmed the land, rather than long-term investment. Eventually this "tax farming" by the army led to the decay of the irrigation systems which was one aspect of a general decline in the empire.

5 The Golden Age of Islam

Under the reign of the Abbasids, the Islamic Empire achieved a brilliant golden age in which Islamic culture spanned three continents. It was a period of the flowering of science and mathematics, art and architecture, literature, and philosophy. During this period, Muslim scholars and scientists made contributions to the world that would have a lasting impact on Western civilization.

The conquests of the Muslims created a vast unified region. Borders that had been closed for a thousand years were open to merchants, pilgrims, and travelers. And people from all over the empire were drawn to Islam's brilliant capital, Baghdad.

SOCIETY DURING THE GOLDEN AGE

The changes brought about by the Abbasids were not just intellectual but social. The Umayyads had maintained the basic tribal pattern of Arabian society. The Umayyad caliphs married Arab women; therefore, their offspring and successors were Arab. The Abbasids, on the other hand, had been brought to power by non-Arabs, and Abbasid caliphs placed no value on keeping their lineage purely Arabian. The caliphs often married foreigners, or had children by concubines and slaves. Rather than being disinherited, those children often succeeded their fathers to the throne. Thus, the Arabian aristocracy was soon displaced by a hierarchy that had little regard for ethnic distinctions. As historian G.E. von Grunebaum explains:

> The difference between Arabs and [non-Arab Muslims] lost the basis of its significance. The faithful were all set at the same distance from the ruler who . . . administered the rule of religion from above his subjects, like a god-king. . . . This alteration in the position of the caliph also put an end to his previous connections with the Arab aristocracy. No one was of equal rank with the Abbasids; for this reason they only married slaves; after [the year] 800 not a single caliph was born the son of a free mother. . . . What held the empire together was no longer the "Arab nation," the Arabs in leading positions, but the dynasty as the administrator

of Islamic unity, ultimately therefore Islam itself.[39]

Although men of diverse ethnic backgrounds found it possible to prosper during the time of the Abbasids, the same could not be said of women. Indeed, women's social status deteriorated under the Abbasids. Women under the Umayyads enjoyed a great degree of freedom, and during the early Abbasid period, women enjoyed the same liberty. Early aristocratic Abbasid women exercised considerable influence in state affairs. There are even records of young Arab women engaging in war and commanding troops, composing poetry, and singing and playing music in social situations.

EDUCATION AND THE MADRASSAS DURING THE GOLDEN AGE

Islamic society placed a high value on education and knowledge, particularly religious knowledge. Education was crucial to Islamic law, and so institutions called madrassas were founded for the study of law and religious science.

The Arabic word *madrasa* is derived from the root meaning "to study." In madrassas students were instructed to live just and wise lives. They learned to perform many religious and legal rites within the community. They were taught the correct path of living by sheikhs, or religious leaders and teachers. The sheikh was chosen by the student or his father because the relationship with the sheikh was considered extremely important. The reputation of the sheikh would later determine the student's career for life.

Education began at an early age with the memorization of the entire Koran. Most students accomplished this by the age of eight and went on to memorize and analyze great works in detail, memorizing four to five hundred lines a day. Once a student had mastered a text, the sheikh gave the student a license, or *ijaza*, allowing him to transmit the knowledge to the next generation.

Although knowledge was heavily emphasized in Islamic tradition, few women were educated in madrassas. According to Islamic principle, "men are the guardians of women because God has set one over the other," so education was set aside primarily for men. Islamic law forbade women from working in civic, legal, or religious occupations, thus making preparation in madrassas unnecessary. Islamic educators also believed that men should not be distracted from their studies by the presence of women. Many women, however, were educated by their fathers, brothers, or husbands, and historical records show that many women memorized the Koran and studied under sheikhs.

A European print presents a stylized portrait of Arab women. By the time of the Abbasids, women were strictly segregated from men and were kept in seclusion.

STRICT SEGREGATION OF WOMEN

However, by the 900s, women were strictly segregated from men and were kept in seclusion. The practice of veiling became mandatory. Veiling had originally been a custom to distinguish free women from slaves. Wearing a veil interfered with work. Gradually, this practice was extended to concealing all parts of a woman's body. The seclusion of women in the harem, rather than allowing them to move freely in society, became mandatory as well. In practice, this meant that women were secluded behind a screen or curtain and required to live in separate quarters from the men. Later, women were so restricted that one Arab writer of the time noted,

> Some of the pious elders (may God be pleased with them) have said that a woman should leave her house on three occasions only: when she is conducted to the house of her bridegroom, on the deaths of her parents, and when she goes to her own grave.[40]

Sexual morals in the empire became lax, and people engaged in excessive luxury. Women came to be regarded as untrustworthy, as portrayed in the collection of stories *The Thousand and One Nights*. This same attitude is reflected in a letter written by Abu Bakr al-Khwarizmi (ca. 993) offering sympathy to a friend who had lost his daughter. In it, the writer implies that morals are so lax that a man might be more fortunate if his daughter dies than if she marries. "We are in an age in which if one of us . . . should marry his daughter to a grave he would acquire thereby the best of sons-in-law."[41]

The ideal of feminine beauty, however, did not change from that held by the Bedouin tribesmen. An Arab writer of the time described the ideal beauty: She should be tall and willowy, "her face as round as the full moon, her hair darker than the night, her cheeks white and rosey with a mole not unlike a drop of ambergris upon a plate of alabaster, her eyes intensely black . . . and large like those of a wild deer, her eyelids drowsy or languid, her mouth small with teeth like pearls set in coral."[42]

Marriage remained a positive value, indeed a duty, and children were considered a blessing from God. Marriages were arranged by families or guardians of the couple and were considered a sacred contract between two families. The official wedding ceremony consisted of an offer of a dowry and its acceptance in front of witnesses. There followed a banquet in which men and women dined separately.

Women's status at home mirrored their reduced status in society at large. Wives' primary duties were to serve their husbands, care for their children, and manage their households. Other duties depended on their social class. The wife of a farmer might help her husband in the fields. A merchant's wife might help in a shop. Upper-class women would direct the servants and slaves and make sure the household ran smoothly.

A woman was, however, accorded respect for her ability to bear children. Yet even this recognition of unique status could work against a woman. If a woman was unable to have children, her husband could divorce her or take an additional wife.

RABI'AH AL 'ADAWIYAH: POET AND MYSTIC

Rabi'ah al 'Adawiyah was born in Basra, Iraq, about 717. According to tradition, Rabi'ah was a poor orphan who was sold into slavery. As a slave, she was kept busy during the day with her duties, but at night she devoted herself to prayer, sleeping only briefly. One night her master saw her at prayer, when a brilliant light miraculously appeared over her. Her master, recognizing her saintliness, freed her.

Rabi'ah spent the rest of her life in Basra, devoted to prayer and meditation. The focus of her devotion was to seek union with God. As her fame spread, many people sought her spiritual guidance. Rabi'ah expressed her love of God in poetry. In the following poem, which is reproduced at the Web site www.sufimaster.org, Rabi'ah asks God for what she considers a just reward:

> O God, if I worship You for fear of Hell, burn me in Hell.
> And if I worship You in hope of Paradise,
> Exclude me from Paradise.
> But if I worship You for Your Own sake,
> Grudge me not Your everlasting Beauty.

Another of her poems expresses her intimate relation with God:

> In your light I learn how to love.
> In your beauty, how to make poems.
> You dance inside my chest,
> Where no one sees you.

Rabi'ah died in 801. Her poetry was collected and passed down by later writers.

In addition to bearing and raising children, a woman's responsibility was looking after the home. In upper-class homes during the reign of the Abbasids, housewives were far removed from the desert Bedouin who lived in camel-hair tents and sat on rugs and cushions. The most important piece of furniture in the home was the divan, or long sofa that extended along three sides of a room. The floors were covered with beautifully woven decorative carpets. Meals were served on decorative trays and platters placed on low wood tables. In wealthier homes the trays were made of silver and the tables were inlaid with tortoise shell or mother-of-pearl.

Both men and women during this period were apt to avail themselves of the refined foods and drink of the civilized world. While their Bedouin ancestors had eaten foods such as beetles, weasels, and scorpions, the people during Abbasid times ate Persian stew and rich sweets, and sweetened sherbet flavored with bananas, roses, or mulberries. Despite the official Islamic prohibition of consuming alcohol, people often indulged in alcoholic beverages. Wine and a drink called *khamr*, made from dates, were the favorites. Drinking parties were common.

CLEANLINESS IS A PART OF FAITH

According to Muslim tradition, cleanliness is a part of faith. Muslims observed this tradition with the use of public baths. Baths were used not only for ceremonial ablutions, or washing, but also as a gathering place for luxurious amusement. In the center of each bathhouse was a large domed chamber with small windows. The central chamber was heated with steam rising from a jet of water. Surrounding the central chamber were smaller, marble-lined rooms, with floors inlaid with mosaics. These rooms were used for lounging, enjoying refreshments, and socializing. The bathhouses, however, were primarily for men's use. In keeping with the Muslim tradition of separating the sexes, special days were reserved for women to use the baths.

For entertainment, indoor games such as backgammon, chess, and dice were common during the Abbasid period. The most famous of the Abbasid

A fifteenth-century painting depicts Muslims at a public bath. These baths served as important gathering places for Muslim men.

caliphs, Harun ar-Rashid, is credited with introducing the game of chess from Persia. The game soon became a favorite of the aristocracy, taking the place of the previous favorite, dice. Outdoor sports were also common, such as archery, polo, fencing, horse racing (accompanied by betting), and—most popular of all—hunting. The Persians introduced falconry and hawking, which became popular later in the Abbasid period. Hawks and falcons were used to hunt gazelles or antelopes, partridges, wild geese, and ducks. Hunting dogs assisted with the big game.

A far less pleasant aspect of life in the Islamic Empire was slavery. Most servants were slaves, non-Muslims. Slaves were captured, taken as prisoners during war, or during peacetime purchased in slave markets. Slaves came from a number of subject peoples. Most were Slavs, Armenians, Berbers, and Greeks. Some slaves were black Africans; still others were Turks. The number of slaves in the empire was enormous. Tens of thousands of captives taken in the various wars and rebellions were enslaved. Although all wealthy persons owned slaves, the caliph was likely the largest slaveholder in the empire. For example, in the palace of Caliph al-Muqtadir (908–932), there were reportedly eleven thousand Greek and Sudanese slaves. Another caliph, al-Mutawakkil, had four thousand slaves that he kept as concubines.

Slaves were sometimes used for delicate missions. For example, the caliph al-Ma'mun used his slaves as spies, presenting them as gifts to individuals he suspected of treason. The slaves would report on the activities of their new owners and kill them if those activities indicated treachery.

The slaves of the empire were not, however, generally used in agricultural work. Still, as servants to the wealthy, slaves contributed enormously to the prosperity of the empire, and allowed many of its citizens the free time to engage in the pursuit of art and learning.

The Magnificence of Baghdad

The center of the grand Islamic Empire during its golden age was the fabled city of Baghdad. The city represented the high point of the Abbasid caliphs' efforts to build a peaceful, prosperous society. Baghdad was built by the caliph al-Mansur in 734. The Islamic historian al-Tabari describes al-Mansur's selection of the site for his new city:

> He came to the area of the bridge and crossed at the present site of Qasr al-Salam. He then prayed the afternoon prayer. It was in summer, and at the site of the palace there was then a priest's church. He spent the night there, and awoke next morning having passed the sweetest and gentlest night on earth. He stayed, and everything he saw pleased him. Then he said, "This is the site on which I shall build. Things can arrive here by way of the Euphrates, Tigris, and a network of canals. Only a place like this will support the army and the general populace." So he laid it out and assigned monies for its construction, and laid

A thirteenth-century illustration depicts an Arab slave market. Slaves in the Islamic Empire were usually non-Muslims taken as prisoners of war or purchased during peacetime.

the first brick with his own hand, saying "in the name of God, and praise to Him. The earth is God's; He causes to inherit of it whom He wills among His servants, and the result thereof is to them that fear Him." Then he said, "Build, and God bless you!"[43]

The site al-Mansur chose was a congenial one in a fertile valley between the Tigris and Euphrates rivers, watered with a series of canals. The surrounding land could produce enough food for a large city. Boats plying the Tigris River brought wheat and barley from the land between the rivers to the north, as well as dates and rice from Basra and other cities to the south. The site also lay near the main land route through the Zagros Mountains into Persia and beyond.

About one hundred thousand craftsmen, laborers, and architects, drawn from around the empire, worked for four years to build the city. Al-Mansur originally named his city Madinat al-Salam (City of Peace), but the village on whose site the city was built had been known as Baghdad since ancient times, and that name continued in use.

Al-Mansur adopted the practice of previous rulers in the region and kept himself apart from those he ruled. Baghdad was designed to create this distance and to reflect the magnificence of its ruler, setting the precedent for the caliphs who came after him. Baghdad was called the "Round City" because of its three circular walls set inside one another. The outermost wall was double thick and surrounded by a moat. Inside it were the houses of administrators and administrative offices. The next area encircled by the middle wall contained the army barracks housing the caliph's personal guards. The innermost wall was ninety feet high. It surrounded the caliph's palace, with its magnificent green dome. Many of the stones for the palace were taken from the

CORDOBA: "THE ORNAMENT OF THE WORLD"

The city of Cordoba in southern Spain rivaled Baghdad as a glorious center of culture and learning during Islam's golden age. Cordoba was the most prosperous and sophisticated city on the European continent. While the rest of Europe was still in the Dark Ages, Cordoba was a city of light. Cities of northern Europe were cold and dark. The European visitors to Cordoba marveled at the city's wide well-paved streets that admitted plenty of sunshine. At night the city was lit with streetlights. It also had abundant fresh running water and gardens overflowing with brilliant flowers. A Saxon nun named Hrosthwita of Gandersheim who visited the city was so overwhelmed with its beauty that she described it as "the ornament of the world."

Cordoba had a population of about 1 million. While in Paris people were living in shacks by the side of the river, ordinary people in Cordoba lived in large houses. There were over 200,000 for ordinary citizens, and 60,000 mansions for the wealthy and important officials. Cordoba was home to the Great Mosque, one of the grandest structures on the European continent at the time. The city also contained 900 public baths, 27 free schools, and a library of more than 400,000 books, at a time when Europe's great Benedictine monastery in Switzerland had only about 600 books. Muslim scholars gathered in Cordoba, and like their counterparts in Baghdad, they made contributions in science, philosophy, and mathematics.

The city's commercial districts housed over 80,000 shops. Its 13,000 weavers produced fine silk and woolen fabrics that were known the world over. Cordoba was also famous for its production of leather. In English, the word *cordovan*, which refers to a fine leather, memorializes the fine leather produced in Cordoba.

ruins of the old Persian capital Ctesiphon, which was located nearby. Four gates were set equidistant in the walls, and radiating from these gates were four highways that connected the center of Islam to all corners of the empire.

At its height, Baghdad was considered the center of not just the empire, but the universe, a city that rivaled ancient Rome and Athens. At the center of the city stood the sumptuous palace of the caliph, who surrounded himself with splendor and ceremony befitting the magnificence of the city. All visitors to the caliph had to be approved by court officials. When the caliph was giving an audience in his throne room, an executioner stood nearby, poised to deliver punishment at the caliph's command.

The caliph's splendid display of wealth and ceremony was meant to intimidate foreign visitors and to impress his own people with his power. Al-Katib al-Baghdadi, a Muslim historian, describes a visit to the caliph by a Byzantine emissary. The emissary was given a tour of the palace and saw the courts and parks, the treasure rooms, the soldiers and chamberlains, and the elephants draped in peacock-blue silk brocade. Then the emissary was taken to see the most wondrous mechanical device in the Room of the Tree, which Al-Katib describes:

A tree stand[s] in the midst of a great circular tank filled with clear water. The tree has eighteen branches, every branch having numerous twigs, on which sit all sorts of gold and silver birds, both large and small. Most of the branches of this tree are of silver, but some are of gold, and they spread into the air carrying leaves of different colours. The leaves of the tree move as the wind blows, while the birds pipe and sing.[44]

According to other reports, "On either side of the tank stood the statues of fifteen horsemen, dressed in brocade and armed with lances, constantly moving as though in combat."[45]

Al-Katib went on to describe the presence of the caliph:

He was arrayed in clothes . . . embroidered in gold being seated on an ebony throne. . . . To the right of the throne hung nine collars of gems . . . and to the left were the like, all of famous jewels. . . . Before the caliph stood five of his sons, three to the right and two to the left.[46]

Beyond the walls of the palace was a city that was large even by standards of the twenty-first century. By A.D. 800 the population of the city numbered as many as a half-million people. Baghdad was also an important commercial center. Around the southern gate merchants set up bazaars and built houses, forming a commercial district known as al-Karkh. Other suburbs grew up on the east bank of the Tigris. A visitor to the city described it in glowing terms: "All the exquisite neighborhoods covered with parks, gardens, villas, and beautiful promenades are filled with bazaars and finely built mosques and baths. They stretch for miles on both sides of the glittering river."[47]

The streets of Baghdad were filled with people from across the empire and beyond: slaves, merchants, visitors, and officials from Europe, Africa, and Asia. The bazaars were filled with a dazzling assortment of rich and exotic goods from every corner of the empire.

Baghdad reached the height of its glory during the reign of Caliph Harun ar-Rashid (786–809). Harun invited poets, artists, musicians, and scholars from all over the empire to his court. Riches flowed into it from all points in the Islamic Empire over land by caravan and over sea by merchant ships. Baghdad was the richest city in the world at that

Built in 734, the magnificent city of Baghdad served as the center of the Islamic Empire during its golden age.

During the empire's golden age, Baghdad was an important commercial center. Vendors in the city's bazaars sold goods from every corner of the known world.

time. It was this prosperous hub of the empire that figures in the collection of stories *The Thousand and One Nights.* The collection includes stories of Aladdin and the Magic Lamp, Ali Baba and the Forty Thieves, and Sinbad the Sailor, who set sail from the port of Basra to the south of Baghdad. Although fiction, these stories give a reader a sense of the rich, exotic city of Baghdad during the empire's golden age.

Baghdad was the center not only of wealth and commerce but of arts and learning as well. The city was a magnet for the best minds and most talented people of the time. People came to Baghdad from all over the empire to work and to exchange ideas. All major innovations of the time came from Baghdad, or came to Baghdad. Fortunately, Baghdad provided a center worthy of all this talent.

Chapter

6 Intellectual and Artistic Achievements of the Golden Age

Modern scholars consider the period of creativity and vitality of the Islamic scholars during the golden age to be one of the most brilliant periods in history. In a center of learning known as the House of Wisdom, the best minds of the empire came together. This coming together of various cultures and ideas produced dramatic achievements in all areas of study.

THE HOUSE OF WISDOM

Many of the grand achievements of the golden age began in the great center of learning in Baghdad—the Bayt al Hikmah, or House of Wisdom, founded by Caliph al-Ma'mun (786–833). The center combined an academy and library. The Δscholars at the House of Wisdom were not specialists in any one field. They were expected to have knowledge in a variety of areas, such as philosophy, mathematics, astronomy, geography, and medicine. The task that al-Ma'mun set before these scholars and scientists of the House of Wisdom was enormous. Al-Ma'mun sent out emissaries to collect manuscripts of important philosophical and scientific works from Greece, Persia,

and India—from every corner of the empire. Many of the manuscripts were in the hands of the Byzantines, with whom the emissaries had to bargain.

Once obtained, the manuscripts were brought back to Baghdad and deposited in the House of Wisdom, where the world's most prominent scholars—Christians and Jews as well as Muslims—were given the task of translating them into Arabic. The House of Wisdom housed a vast library of works, representing the collective artistic and scholarly labor of human civilization.

The Muslims' labor in passing on these ideas was just as important to human civilization as the labor of developing the ideas in the first place. As Hitti observes, "Had the researches of [Greek philosopher] Aristotle, [physician] Galen and [astronomer] Ptolemy been lost to posterity the world would have been as poor as if they had never been produced."[48]

The Arabic translations of these works spread to other centers of learning in the Islamic Empire, made possible by a product previously unknown in that part of the world. In the mid-700s, when Arab armies reached central Asia, they had encountered paper, which was in use in China. The use of paper quickly spread throughout the Islamic world, and it was paper that allowed the transmission of knowledge throughout the empire. In Baghdad, all the ancient knowledge that had been translated and all the new writings by scholars at the House of Wisdom were copied down in books by hundreds of scribes. In the Baghdad marketplace, there was a street of booksellers that had over a hundred shops, all selling books and paper. By contrast, in Europe at the same time, Christian monks were copying manuscripts on parchment, which was made from animal skins. Monasteries were lucky to own five or ten books.

The development of paper and books allowed the knowledge accumulated by the scholars in the House of Wisdom to spread through the Islamic world. Since the books were in Arabic, that language emerged as the language of learning and culture throughout the empire. Eventually, not only did Europeans learn the use of paper from the Muslims, but the books that were translated from Arabic into Latin spread throughout Europe, sowing the seeds of the European Renaissance.

SCIENCE AND MATHEMATICS

Once Muslims had gathered and translated the knowledge from the ancients, they brought to it the spirit of questioning, challenging the ideas in the texts and testing their truth. Caliph al-Ma'mun was also interested in developing the sciences. He established observatories where Muslim scholars tested the knowledge of astronomy that they had recovered from the ancients.

ISLAMIC LAW: ULEMA AND SHARIA

As the empire grew more complex, religious leaders found that they needed something more than the simple traditions of desert Arabs to guide their religious and moral decisions. Actively sponsored by the Abbasids, religious scholars and jurists emerged who interpreted the Koran and the sunna and applied those interpretations to the law. Over time, they built up a body of law based on their work. These men were known as the ulema, and they developed the legal system known as sharia. The Muslims saw the law of God and the law of humans as strands in the same tapestry—both social law and religious law were one. Thus religion and politics are intertwined in the same fabric of human society.

The sharia covered all aspects of individual behavior, including marriage, divorce, business practices, religious observances, and property rights. The sharia also included the acceptable practices to be followed by the Islamic government and the caliph. The sacred law of the sharia helped unify society in the Muslim world.

Muslim mathematicians and scientists also developed new works. Muslims introduced the Indian number system, including the concept of zero and of decimal points. They also developed the system of counting known as Arabic numerals, which would be used throughout the world from then on.

One scientist who was a typical scholar working in the House of Wisdom was Muhammad ibn Musa al-Khwarizmi. He drew on Indian and Greek studies in astronomy to produce astronomical tables that would form the basis for later Western research. Al-Khwarizmi's most important contribution is in mathematics—his famous work titled *The Book of Integration and Equation* was the basis of a new branch of mathematics. Part of the Arabic title of his book is *al-jabr*, which eventually became *algebra* in English. Using an ancient navigational tool the Arabs had rediscovered, al-Khwarizmi also created an important geography book, *The Image of the Earth*, which contained regional maps of the empire that were more accurate than those previously available. This helped not only merchants but other travelers as well as they crossed the vast Islamic Empire.

House of Wisdom scholars also made original contributions to geometry, as well as translating the works of Greek mathematicians such as Euclid. The Islamic historian Ibn Khaldun believed, in fact, that the study of geometry was of special importance, since in his words, "it enlightens the intelligence of the man who cultivates it and gives him a habit of thinking exactly."[49]

A sixteenth-century manuscript depicts a team of Muslim astronomers. During Islam's golden age, several observatories were established throughout the empire.

ISLAMIC MEDICINE

The greatest scientific achievements of the Islamic Empire, however, came in medicine. This was in keeping with the teachings of Islam, which encourage pious Muslims to care for the poor and sick. Scholars at the House of Wisdom translated into Arabic many of the ancient Greek medical texts. In addition, Muslim physicians added to the body of medical information. At a time when Europeans were relying on prayer for health and healing, Muslim physicians had concluded that disease was transmitted by tiny airborne organisms. (Not until the middle of the nineteenth century would Europeans accept what is called the germ theory of disease.) Based on their theory, Muslim doctors determined that sick patients should be quarantined and treated separately from well persons.

This practice led Muslims to develop the first effective hospitals, where different diseases were treated in separate wards. These hospitals were often built by wealthy donors in honor of Allah. Treatment in the hospitals was free.

Muslim hospitals treated a variety of illnesses and injuries. Even mental illness was treated. These hospitals were often teaching hospitals, with separate rooms where medical students attended classes taught by some of the foremost physicians in the empire. An understanding of drugs was essential in treating patients, and it was during the Islamic Empire's golden age that Muslims established the first school of pharmacy.

Muslim physicians and scientists were also interested in light and the structure of the eye. Their study of optics led to developments in treatment for diseases of the eye, which were common in the sunny climate of the Middle East. Muslim doctors were the first to surgically remove cataracts, an area of cloudiness in the lens of the eye that eventually causes blindness.

Government officials kept close watch over the practice of medicine in the empire. As early as the ninth century, physicians and pharmacists were required to pass exams. Officials also were interested in public health and hygiene, and they established public health practices that were unknown to the rest of the world. Public health was so important that in the tenth century groups of physicians were organized to go place to place to treat the sick. Some physicians even regularly visited prisons, treating the inmates.

The Islamic Empire produced a number of famous physicians. One example is Ibn Razi (865–925), also known as Rhazes. A story is told of how Ibn Razi chose the site for a new hospital. The story goes that Ibn Razi went to several places in the city of Baghdad, leaving pieces of raw meat at each location. He later returned to the sites where he had left the meat, and chose the place where the meat had remained fresher, with the least decay. He reasoned that this place would be the healthiest location.

Another famous physician—one of the best known names in Islamic medical science—was Ibn Sina (980–1037), known to the West as Avicenna. His most important work, *The Canon of Medicine*, brought together the medical knowledge of the ancient Greeks and the new discoveries

A Muslim doctor attends to a patient in this manuscript page. Some of Islam's greatest scientific achievements were in medicine.

of Muslim physicians. His book was used as a standard medical textbook in Europe for six centuries.

Over time, an enormous body of knowledge in the sciences was built up. Eventually, the Greek works that had been translated into Arabic and the Islamic studies in medicine and pharmacology were translated into Latin and passed on to western Europe. This medical knowledge and practice passed on by the Islamic Empire would form the basis for centuries of European medical study and practice.

ISLAMIC LITERATURE

Though science and mathematics were the most important contributions of the Islamic Empire, literature was also a central part of the golden age. The centerpiece of Islamic literature was—and remains to this day—the Koran. Not only is it considered the true word of God as revealed to Muhammad, but it is considered the reproduction on earth of the original word of God. Beyond that, the Arabic language in which it was revealed

AVICENNA

The medical knowledge of the Islamic Empire far exceeded the knowledge and practice of medieval Europe, and Muslim physicians and scientists were responsible for some of the most important advances in medical knowledge. It was a Muslim physician who first distinguished measles from smallpox. A famous Muslim surgeon, Al Zahrawi, discovered how to cauterize wounds, or burn them with a hot iron to prevent infection.

Muslim science reached its peak with its most famous physician, Abu Ali al-Husayn ibn Abd Allah ibn Sina, also known by his Latin name, Avicenna. Ibn Sina was born in Persia in 980 and died there fifty-seven years later. When Ibn Sina was seventeen years old, he cured the king of Bukhara of an illness said to be incurable by all other doctors. As his reward he was granted permission to study in the king's library, which contained ancient works by authors such as Aristotle.

Ibn Sina spent much of his life traveling throughout the Islamic Empire acting as a doctor and a teacher. He was the first physician to detail the distinct parts of the eye. Much of his work concerned the eye because many Arabs were afflicted with eye problems caused by the bright sun and blowing sand. Ibn Sina studied how muscles and nerves work in the body and how nerves perceive pain. He also studied how disease is passed on to people, and he discovered that tuberculosis is a contagious disease. Ibn Sina believed in the relationship between psychology and health, understanding that emotions could cause illness.

Ibn Sina contributed a wealth of medical knowledge to the medieval world. He wrote many books, some of which were translated into Latin and used as medical texts in western Europe for centuries. His book *The Canon of Medicine* detailed medical thought at the time and included over 750 pharmaceutical drugs for use in treating illnesses. It covered all aspects of medicine and is considered the most famous single book in medical history.

is considered to be the purest and most beautiful expression possible.

Besides being considered unsurpassable as a work of literature, the Koran was the foundation of education. As historian F.E. Peters explains:

> A Muslim's education arose from the simple [command] to read and understand the Qur'an, and the developed literary sciences, whether [related to the study of language] or [related to the art of language], had their common roots in the Arabic Qur'an, which was at once the sacred word of Allah and a miracle of perfection.[50]

The Koran was seen as perfect in its form, as revealed in the Arabic language. To translate it to another language would be to make it imperfect. Therefore, it was recited only in Arabic, and Islam's conquered peoples learned to recite the Koran in Arabic. As a result, eventually Arabic became the language of literature and learning throughout the empire.

Of all the literary forms, the most popular was poetry. Arabs had a long tradition of poetry dating to pre-Islamic times. During the golden age, the caliphs became great patrons of the arts, inviting poets from around the empire to their courts. The rhythmic and intricate Arabic *qasidah*, or ode, from pre-Islamic times remained popular. While Arabic was the dominant language, poets also composed in the Persian language. The Persian poet most well known to Europeans is Omar Khayyám, whose verses are known to English speakers as the *Rubaiyat*, which was translated into English in the mid-1800s by the British poet Edward FitzGerald.

A group of men discusses the Koran. Muslims believe the Koran to be the true word of God as revealed to Muhammad.

POETRY IN ANDALUSIA

Poetry had always played an important part in the culture of the Arabs. One of the most famous poets of Andalusia (Muslim Spain) was Ibn Zaydun (1003–1071), who grew up in Cordoba but was forced to leave his beloved city. The following poem (found in Hourani's *History of the Arab Peoples*) expresses the longing he feels when recalling his youth in Cordoba.

> God has sent showers upon the abandoned dwelling-places of those we loved. He has woven upon them a striped, many-coloured garment of flowers, and raised among them a flower like a star. How many girls like images trailed their garments among such flowers, when life was fresh and time was at our service. . . . How happy they were, those days that have passed, days of pleasure, when we lived with those who had black flowing hair and white shoulders. . . . Now say to Destiny whose favours have vanished—favours I have lamented as the nights have passed—how faintly its breeze has touched me in my evening. But for him who walks in the night the stars will shine: greetings to you Cordoba, with love and longing.

Short stories were popular as well. One work of literature from the golden age that is well known to Westerners is the collection of tales known as *The Thousand and One Nights*. The folktales were compiled from various cultures within the empire—Indian, Persian, and Egyptian as well as Arabian. The collection is set within what is called a frame story—that is, a story that surrounds the collection of tales and links them together. In the case of *The Thousand and One Nights*, the frame story is of a young woman, Scheherazade, who tells a story each night to her husband, the king. The stories she tells contain characters familiar to Westerners such as Aladdin, Sinbad the Sailor, and Ali Baba. These folk tales reflect the wide diversity of traditions brought together under the Islamic Empire.

ARCHITECTURE AND ENGINEERING

Islamic architecture, which was characterized by the great dome, celebrated the bringing together of diverse traditions under the empire. Like the empire itself, which encircled the known world and included many cultures within it, the domes of buildings surrounded the interior space of the building. Buildings were decorated both inside and out with intricate stonework and elaborate designs in tile of interweaving leaves and flowers.

Baghdad's great palaces, libraries, hospitals, and mosques, often surrounded by lovely Persian gardens, are depicted in accounts written during the golden age, but the structures themselves have long since been destroyed in wars and by natural causes. Not even rubble remains to mark the places where they once stood. However, the splendor of the golden age of Islamic architecture can still be seen in the city of Cordoba in southern Spain—the westernmost part of the Islamic world during the golden age.

The glory of Cordoba was its Great Mosque (which was converted to a Roman Catholic cathedral in the thirteenth century), one of the largest sacred buildings in all of Islam. The building is a vast rectangle 590 by 425 feet, and contains a large courtyard. The roof of the sanctuary is supported by some 850 pillars, all made of marble, porphyry, and jasper of various colors rising from a marble floor. The pillars are in rows, with each row supporting a tier of open horseshoe-shaped arches. The arches are constructed of alternating vertical rows of red and white bricks, producing a striking effect. Interlacing ribbed vaults were used in the construction, which most historians believe was later imitated for use in the Christian Gothic cathedrals of Europe.

The most splendid decoration in the Great Mosque is in the mihrab, or prayer niche. The mihrab was a standard feature of Muslim mosques. It was built to show the faithful the appropriate direction to face (toward Mecca) during prayers. The mihrab came to occupy an especially sacred place, worthy of the most beautiful decoration. In the mosque of Cordoba, the mihrab is a small octagonal recess whose roof is a single block of white marble carved in the shape of a shell. Its sides are inlaid with gold and mosaics.

The Great Mosque of Cordoba was originally built in 784–786, and additions were made to the structure through the ninth and tenth centuries. This was a time when the rest of Europe was struggling through the period known as the Dark Ages, before any of the European cities had become great urban centers and before any of the great cathedrals of Europe were begun. The few Europeans who visited the city of Cordoba and saw the Great Mosque were amazed at the beauty and luxury of this masterpiece of Islamic architecture.

Building the great mosques and palaces of Islam required incredible engineering skills, but Muslim engineers used their skills elsewhere as well. To the Muslims, who had originally come from the parched deserts of Arabia, water was considered a great luxury. They enjoyed being surrounded by running water in the form of streams and fountains. Thus most luxurious palaces had courtyards with fountains and pools, and often running streams.

The interest in water meant that much of Muslim engineering was related to the movement and control of water. Muslims, for example, perfected the waterwheel. They also built elaborate underground channels called *qanats* to carry water to cities. The channels were built about fifty feet below the surface of the earth and tapped underground water supplies. The channels had to be very slightly inclined

A congregation of Muslims kneels in prayer inside the Great Mosque of Cordoba. The mosque is considered a masterpiece of Islamic architecture.

downhill over long distances so that the water would flow of its own accord. Manholes were built in the channels so that they could be cleaned and maintained.

ART

The great buildings of the Islamic Empire depended on Islamic artists for their elaborate decoration. The Koran provided the inspiration for much of Muslim art. Islam discouraged the depiction of animal and human images, since Muslims considered it blasphemous to make "graven images" of humans or animals. Instead of such depictions, decorative architectural art usually included complex geometric shapes and intricate floral patterns.

Mosques were usually decorated with verses from the Koran written in ornate script. The walls of mosques would have Koranic verses written in gold, or captured in carved stone or in mosaic tile. Calligraphy, as ornamental writing is called, became a high art, and verses from the Koran written in this way were used to decorate many objects. Scarves or other clothing made of fine silk might have verses woven in gold thread along the edges. Koranic verses might also be used to decorate the pages of books or the walls of homes and palaces.

The exceptions to the general prohibition against human and animal imagery occurred in Persian-influenced art. In pre-Islamic Persia there was a strong tradition of miniature painting that depicted hunters and warriors and legendary beasts. Under Islam, Persian artists continued this tradition of miniatures with excruciatingly fine detail, sometimes applying paint using a single hair. These paintings often appeared as illustrations in manuscripts.

Muslim artists and artisans expressed their talent in a variety of other ways as well. Art historians consider textiles from the Islamic golden age to be some of the finest ever created. Artisans in Syrian towns

Muslim engineers, applying their knowledge to the dynamics of water movement, perfected the waterwheel.

The walls of Islamic mosques were usually decorated with carved stone, calligraphy, or ornate mosaic tiles like these.

created beautiful glass noted for its clarity and delicacy, and it was in great demand as a luxury item. Syrian glass with enameled inscriptions was used in the palaces and mosques. Also in demand for exterior and interior decoration of buildings were mosaic tiles made in Damascus. These glazed square or hexagonal tiles in deep blue, turquoise blue, and green sometimes also had images of flowers.

Jewelry was also popular during the goldge age. Jewelers cut fine gems for royalty and for wealthy commoners as well. One of the best-known jewels was a large ruby, once owned by Persian monarchs, on which Caliph Harun had his name inscribed. Reportedly the gem was

so brilliant that one writer of the time said that "if it were put in the night-time in a dark room it would shine like a lamp."[51]

THE DECLINE OF THE GOLDEN AGE

As with high points of all civilizations, the golden age of Islam did not last. Civil strife in the form of rebellions and internal divisions weakened the power of the caliphs. The golden age of Islam, whose fountainhead was the deserts of Arabia, faded from view. Yet the legacy of that age would continue to influence Western civilization for more than a thousand years.

7 The Rise of Regional Dynasties

The Islamic empire developed so quickly and was so vast that it was nearly impossible for one person to retain control. The caliph had to give governors of distant provinces power to make decisions on his behalf. Even though the caliph had a system of spies, and he attempted to control his governors, many were able to build up their own power and pass that on to their descendants. Over time, several regional dynasties arose and broke away from the central government. As a result, the power of the Abbasid dynasty declined, until its final destruction in 1258 at the hands of Mongol invaders.

The great distances spanned by the empire enabled distant provinces to ignore the rule of Baghdad. In Tunisia, on the North African coast, the regional authority set himself up as ruler, refusing altogether to acknowledge the power of the caliph of Baghdad. In fact, the Abbasids had no sooner gained power than decentralization began. As Hitti describes,

> About 820 more extensive authority was concentrated in the hands of one man, the caliph of Baghdad, than in those of any other living person; by 920 the power of his successor had so diminished that it was hardly felt even in his capital city. By 1258 the city itself lay in ruins. With its fall Arab [domination] was lost forever and the history of the real caliphate closed.[52]

In Khorasan, a similar weakening of the caliph's authority had even more serious consequences. Khorasan had long been a source of army troops. Its loss forced the Abbasid caliphs to employ Turkish slaves known as Mamluks, who were trained in the military arts. The Turkish troops, who had no loyalty to the government by which they were hired, would eventually grow so powerful that they could appoint and dismiss the caliphs at their whim.

UMAYYAD SPAIN

On coming to power in 749, the Abbasids had attempted to eliminate a potential rival by murdering every member of the Umayyad family. However, one Umayyad prince escaped and in 756 established himself as the ruler in southern Spain, or what the Muslims called Andalusia. The first Umayyad rulers in Spain referred to themselves as provincial governors and at least paid lip service to the caliph's supremacy. For example, a long-standing Muslim custom was to recite the public Friday prayers at the mosque in the name of the caliph, an acknowledgment of his authority. The Spanish Umayyads continued to do this until the reign of Abd ar-Rahman II (912–961). In 929 he began to call himself caliph and have his name used in the Friday prayers, which was a claim of his independence from Abbasid authority.

Under Abd ar-Rahman, Umayyad Spain shared in the empire's golden age, with the capital city of Cordoba rivaling the beauty and elegance of Baghdad. Abd ar-Rahman presided over a period of peace, which drew people from various ethnic backgrounds to the region. Christians and Jews were treated with tolerance by the Muslim rulers, and intellectual and artistic

To acknowledge the caliph's authority, Muslims across the empire recited the Friday prayers in his name.

The Escape of Abd ar-Rahman

When the Abbasids took power, they massacred hundreds of Umayyad princes throughout Syria and Palestine. Only one Umayyad prince survived, Abd ar-Rahman. He escaped the Abbasid soldiers searching for him and made his way to North Africa and from there to Spain. Muslim annals include a description of his historic escape purportedly written by Abd ar-Rahman himself (and quoted in historian Wilson Bishai's *Islamic History of the Middle East*).

> When we were promised security and then deceived at the river of Abu Fadras, I received news of the orders to spill our blood. With the feelings of an outcast, I returned to my home in desperation trying to find a way to save myself and my household. Extremely fearful, I walked out till I reached a village on the Euphrates known for its trees and shrubs. While there, my son Sulayman, who was then only four years old, was playing with me. He left me for a short while then returned crying with fear, hanging onto me as I was pushing him away. Finally I went outside to find out what was the matter and discovered that the whole village was in turmoil as the black banners (of the Abbasids) were unfurled everywhere. My younger brother said to me, "Escape! Escape! These are the black banners!" I took some money with me and escaped with my brother after telling the rest of my family about my intentions, requesting them to send my bondman Badr after me. Accordingly, when the horsemen reached the village, they could not find me. I met one of my acquaintances and asked him to buy for me some beasts of burden and other necessities; but he informed the governor Abd-Allah against me. When he (the governor) came after me, we fled on foot as his horsemen followed. We crossed through some orchards toward the Euphrates, preceding the horsemen to the river, where we swam. The horsemen promised us safe conduct if we returned, but I did not go back. My brother, however, could not persevere in swimming, and believing in their safety promises, he returned. Albeit, they murdered him while I was watching—he was thirteen years old. I bore my grief for him and continued on my way till I disappeared from sight. I hid till they stopped searching for me; then I came out of hiding and started on my trip to North Africa.

life flourished. Christian, Jewish, and Muslim scholars at the university in Cordoba translated Greek texts and new works in mathematics and the sciences that had been produced in Baghdad and elsewhere in the Muslim world. Many of these texts were translated into Latin, which was the language of scholars elsewhere in Europe.

Although the rulers of Andalusia were politically independent of the caliph in Baghdad, culturally Umayyad Spain was an integral part of the greater Islamic world. Islam and the Arabic language linked southern Spain to the rest of the empire. Moreover, despite political differences, people from Cordoba, Baghdad, or any other provincial capital could all meet freely in Mecca during the hajj.

The Umayyad caliphate in Spain began a decline after the death in 1002 of Caliph al-Mansur, who, according to Hitti, was "possibly the greatest statesman and general of Arab Spain."[53] By 1031 the Spanish Umayyad caliphate had disappeared entirely, replaced by splinter kingdoms and principalities, all at odds with one another. The last of the Muslim rulers in Spain was driven out in 1492 after the fall of the city of Granada to Christians.

Spain's moves toward greater independence from the central government of the Islamic Empire were largely political in nature. However, despite the fact that the religion of Islam was the source of the empire's unity, some of the independence movements had their roots in religious differences.

THE FATIMIDS

In the Maghreb (the region of North Africa that borders the Mediterranean Sea) a sect of Shiite Muslims known as Ismaili spread their teachings with missionary zeal. Ismaili believers had long opposed the Abbasid dynasty, which they considered too worldy. Ismailis preached that a religious leader would come who

would restore justice and piety to Islam. A leader named Ubayd Allah (909–934) appeared and claimed to be a descendant of Ali and Fatima, the daughter of Muhammad. He and his followers became known as Fatimids. The Fatimids extended their control over North Africa and then turned their attention to Egypt. Their ultimate goal was the destruction of the Abbasids and installation of the Fatimids as the true leaders of Islam. By 909 they were established in Tunisia and on the Mediterranean island of Sicily. By 969 the Fatimids had captured Egypt, where they established the city of Cairo.

The Fatimid caliphate reached its height under the peaceful reign of Abu Mansur al-Aziz (975–996). His name was recited at Friday prayers all across North Africa from the shores of the Atlantic to the edge of the Red Sea, in Egypt, and in southern Arabia and the cities of Mecca and Damascus. Jerusalem, with its holy shrine, the Dome of the Rock, and the al-Aqsa Mosque was also under Fatimid rule. At least in name, al-Aziz was master of all that region, and the greatest rival of Baghdad. Al-Aziz was so sure that the Fatimids would eventually capture Baghdad that he built a lavish palace in Cairo in which to keep the Abbasids after Baghdad fell. Like previous Fatimids, he also hoped to capture Umayyad Spain. The caliph of Cordoba was not easily intimidated, however. When al-Aziz sent him a rude note, the caliph responded tartly, "[You ridicule] us because [you have] heard of us. If we had ever heard of [you], we would reply."[54]

The Fatimid caliph who followed al-Aziz was Abu Ali Mansur al-Hakim (996–1021), who is considered by historians to have been mentally deranged. Although Jews and Christians for the most part had enjoyed protection under Muslim rulers, al-Hakim decreed that Jews and Christians must wear black clothing and could not ride horses or camels, only donkeys. Al-Hakim's most fateful act was destroying Christian churches, including the Church of the Holy Sepulcher that Christians believed marked the site where Jesus was taken after his crucifixion and from which he arose from the dead. Even though later caliphs rebuilt the church, European Christians were horrified at what they considered the sacrilegious destruction of their holy sites. These acts motivated the later invasion of the Holy Land by Christian crusaders.

Fatimid power and territory gradually shrank over the centuries. By the eleventh century the court was reduced to constant intrigues and fighting between viziers and factions of the army. Repeated plagues and famines in Egypt damaged the peasants' ability to produce food. Taxes were increased as the economy continually worsened. Matters were complicated by the arrival of the Christian crusaders from Europe and the attempts of Amalric, the crusader king of Jerusalem, to conquer Egypt. Finally, in 1171, the last Fatimid throne was taken over by a Muslim military leader known as Saladin.

DECLINE OF THE ABBASIDS

Meanwhile, the effects of hiring non-Arab mercenaries were being felt. The Abbasids had come to power with the help of Persian soldiers-for-hire from Khorasan, rather than Arab soldiers. The early Abbasid caliphs used Persian bodyguards as well. The Arabs made up two divisions, but the Persians were predominant. A later caliph, al-Mutasim, added Turkish troops from central Asia, who had originally been his slaves. The people of Baghdad so resented the alien Turks that the caliph resorted to building a new capital in Samarra in 836 and transferring his government there. The introduction of alien troops eventually caused political instability. In 861 the caliph al-Mutawakkil was assassinated by his Turkish troops, and for nine years the Turkish soldiers made and deposed caliphs as they saw fit. An Arab poet describes the condition of the caliph who succeeded al-Mutawakkil:

> A caliph in a cage between Wasif and Bugha [the Turkish assassins], He repeats whatever they tell him exactly as the parrot does.[55]

The seat of government was eventually returned to Baghdad in 892, but the Turks remained an important force in the later Islamic Empire.

As the empire splintered, the caliph in Baghdad had to rely more and more on his military, and the military in turn grew more and more independent and powerful. The Buwayids were a family of Shia military leaders who came from the edges of the Caspian Sea and claimed descent from the ancient Persian kings. Having already gained control of a number of provinces, they took control of Baghdad itself in 945. Although they allowed the caliph to keep his name and rank, they held the real power of government.

The minaret of the mosque at Samarra still stands in Iraq. In 836 the caliph transferred the empire's capital from Baghdad to Samarra.

In 946 the caliph was accused of plotting against the Buwayids. The preeminent Buwayid leader, Adud ad-Dawlah (949–983), had the caliph paraded through the streets to ad-Dawlah's new palace. There the caliph was blinded—both a practical and symbolic act that made the ruler unable to carry out his duties. The blinding of the caliph marked the real collapse of the Abbasid caliphate, although they continued as figureheads, as the Buwayids made and unmade caliphs at will.

Relative peace and security were established under the Buwayids, the economy improved, and scholarship flourished. Adud ad-Dawlah united the splintered kingdoms that had arisen in Iraq and Persia, creating a state nearly the size of an

MUSLIMS AND THE WEST

Although Muslims and Europeans were geographic neighbors and shared a common Judeo-Christian religious tradition, they remained uneasy with one another. During the period of Muslim expansion, Muslim armies attacked Europe, burning villages, sacking monasteries, and capturing people to sell into slavery. Christian Europeans developed a deep bitterness toward Muslims.

Religion also divided Christians and Muslims. Christians were intolerant of anyone who denied the divinity of Jesus Christ. Christian theologians, church councils, and even the pope condemned the Muslims. For their part, the Muslims considered Christianity as an inferior religion, just a step on the way to the true and final revelations of the prophet Muhammad.

Muslims also considered Europeans culturally inferior. In Muslim eyes, Europeans were dirty, crude, and unlearned, and their medical practices were barbaric. One Muslim account of the difference between Muslim and European medicine describes how a Muslim physician who was called to a crusader encampment treated a knight with an abscessed leg by making a poultice to draw the abscess. When a European physician arrived to treat the same patient, he prescribed amputation of the leg. The helpless Muslim physician stood by as the knight's leg was hacked off with an ax, causing the knight to die almost immediately.

Christians and Jews were tolerated and lived peacefully in the Islamic world, where there were Christian churches and places of worship for Jews. Muslims, however, had a fear of traveling in Europe, where there were no mosques, acceptable food, or other things necessary to the Muslim way of life. Muslims preferred to send Jewish or Christian representatives when it was necessary for them to do business in Europe. Thus, the people of the medieval world's two great cultural traditions—Christendom and Islam—remained strangers, a legacy whose effects are still felt today.

empire once again. Ad-Dawlah married the daughter of the caliph, and had the caliph marry his daughter, which cemented the ties of the families and gave the Buwayids a legitimate claim to succession of the Abbasid caliphate.

Ad-Dawlah, who took the title *sha-hanshah*, ruled from his capital in Shiraz, in what today is south-central Iran. He restored the beauty of Baghdad, which had suffered from the previous occupations and neglect. He built a hospital staffed with twenty-four physicians, who also conducted classes for medical students. The Buwayids were Shiites, and ad-Dawlah built a shrine on the site of the tomb of Ali, whom the Shiite Muslims honored. He also restored Christian churches and monasteries in Baghdad and built an academy stocked with ten thousand books.

Feuding among various factions of the Buwayids, and the resentment of the Sunnis in Baghdad against the Shiite Buwayids, led to their downfall. The Buwayid power was weakened, and in 1055, invading Turks entered Baghdad and ended Buwayid rule.

SELJUK TURKS

The conqueror of Baghdad was Tughril Beg, part of a dynasty known as the Seljuks. When the Seljuk Turks took power, the caliph in Baghdad was only a shadow of the previous Abbasid caliphs who had wielded real power. The caliph's empire was centered in Baghdad and there was no hope of regaining power over the Umayyads of Spain or the Fatimids of Cairo and North Africa. Arab chieftains held small pieces of territories in northern Syria and regions in what is now northern Iraq. Persia and lands to the east were divided into small pieces ruled by Persian princes and petty kings, all ready to do battle with one another at the slightest excuse.

The wild Turkish tribesmen, while conquerors, also brought new blood into the waning Islamic Empire. They soon adopted the religion of Islam, and they took the title of sultan. The Seljuks expanded their rule, and by 1072 had captured most of Syria from the Fatimids, including the city of Damascus. They eventually ruled an empire that stretched from Syria to central Asia.

Under the Seljuks, the caliphs continued to be mere figureheads. Even though in theory the caliphs were the source of authority in the Islamic world, the sultans actually ruled. In 1122 Caliph al-Mustarshid attempted to throw off Seljuk rule but was captured and put to death. His son tried again, but he too failed and was forced to step down. The Abbasid caliphate was again under the firm control of the Seljuk Turks, who remained in control until the Seljuk sultans were themselves finally overthrown in 1181 by Persian rebels.

THE CRUSADERS

In 1097, while the Seljuks held power in Baghdad, the first crusaders from Europe reached Syria. At the time, the Islamic Empire was in one of its most splintered periods. In the eastern part of the empire, the Seljuk sultan was facing problems from revolutionaries, among other troubles, and was not able to take much action against the Christian invaders. In the west, the Fatimid caliphate in Egypt was weak and in decline as well. The crusaders were able to take the city of Antioch, in Syria, and from there they took what they considered the greatest prize—Jerusalem.

The crusaders never advanced much beyond the coastal regions of Palestine and Syria, where they fortified themselves in massive castles. Interactions between crusaders and Arabs were not a constant state of warfare, however. Because the crusaders had to rely on locals for food and supplies, they learned to interact with the local people, in some cases marrying Arabs and adopting their habits and tastes.

Eventually, however, Syrian Muslims united to drive the crusaders out. The family of Zangi, a Turkish slave acting as a Seljuk representative, extended control into northern Syria. Zangi's son Nur ad-Din mustered support from the cities and from the military for a jihad, or holy war, against the Christians. According to scholar P.H. Newby, Nur ad-Din was

> the ideal Muslim prince; devout, a great believer in the equality of all men before God and the law, of simple even austere tastes, and a good soldier. It was in his time that the idea of recovering Jerusalem so that it could be purified of the unbelievers gained momentum.[56]

Nur ad-Din was so determined to capture Jerusalem and its sacred places that, according to Newby, he "ordered a pulpit to be made against the day he entered Jerusalem in triumph and could install it in the Al-Aqsa Mosque."[57]

However, it would be the most famous of Muslim heroes—Saladin—who would win Jerusalem. Salah ad-Din, or Saladin as he is known to the world, began his military career under Nur ad-Din. He became commander of Syrian troops in Egypt and vizier of Egypt's Fatimid caliph. Saladin, a Sunni Muslim, then abolished the Shiite Fatimid caliphate, returned Egypt to Sunni Islam, and became Egypt's sole ruler. With skillful diplomacy he united all of Syria, northern Mesopotamia, Palestine, and Egypt. Saladin was able to unite military forces behind him, and in 1187 he defeated and destroyed a crusader army and captured the city of Jerusalem. In contrast to the crusaders, who had slaughtered the inhabitants of Jerusalem when they captured it, Saladin's victory was marked by the generous and humane treatment he gave the people of Jerusalem.

Saladin's victory shocked the West and inspired another Crusade, this one bringing Saladin's most famous opponent, England's King Richard I, known as Richard the Lion Heart. Saladin was able to withstand the onslaught of Christendom's greatest champions, despite his tired and unwilling troops who would fight only for a limited time each year. The crusaders never recaptured Jerusalem, and King Richard departed in 1192.

Saladin died in 1193. His family ruled over the lands he had united as the Ayyubid dynasty until they were overthrown by the Mamluks in 1250.

THE MONGOLS AND THE FALL OF BAGHDAD

In 1258 the city of Baghdad, and the Islamic caliphs, received a deathblow. The Mongol leader Hulegu, a descendant of the powerful Mongol conqueror Genghis Khan, marched westward from central Asia to carve an empire for himself. Hulegu sent a message to Caliph al-Musta'sim in Baghdad to surrender the city and demolish its outer walls. The caliph refused, and in January 1258 Hulegu attacked the city walls using mangonels, medieval war machines that hurled heavy stones. The frightened authorities sent the vizier to ask for terms of surrender, but Hulegu refused to

Muslim warriors ambush an army of crusaders. Under Nur ad-Din and Salah ad-Din, the Muslim armies managed to repel the crusaders.

SALADIN AND RICHARD THE LION HEART

The two most famous figures from the era of the Crusades were the two noble enemies Saladin, the Muslim defender of the Holy Land, and Richard, the crusader king of England who had come to recapture Jerusalem.

Actually, the two never met. When Richard arrived in Palestine, one of his first acts was to send a note to Saladin asking for a personal meeting. As Quoted in P.H. Newby's *Saladin in His Time*, Saladin replied, "It is not customary for kings to meet unless they have previously laid the foundations of a treaty; for after they have spoken together . . . it is not seemly for them to make war upon one another." Although Saladin and Richard never met, Saladin's brother al-Adil became friends with Richard.

Saladin and Richard developed a mutual respect, and they exchanged ceremonial gifts. Both were powerful leaders, but with entirely different styles of leadership. Richard was bold and brash, riding at the head of his army and fighting at close quarters with sword and ax. Saladin acted more like a general; he observed the fighting from a vantage point, the better to direct his troops.

While Saladin admired the king, he said of Richard, "He often runs unnecessary dangers and is too [careless] of his life. . . . I would rather be gifted with wealth, so long as it is accompanied by wisdom and moderation, than with boldness and immoderation."

see him. They warned Hulegu that "if the caliph is killed the whole universe is disorganized, the sun hides its face, rain ceases and plants grow no more."[58]

Hulegu was not impressed. His war machines breached the walls, and his hordes swarmed into the city. The caliph, his advisers, and his family were taken prisoner and put to death a few days later. According to historian von Grunebaum, tradition has it that the caliph "was wrapped in a carpet and shaken to death; for had a drop of his blood touched the earth, the world would have begun to shake."[59] The death of the caliph affected all of Islam. As Philip Hitti explains, "For the first time in its history the Muslim world was left without a caliph whose name could be cited in the Friday prayers."[60] The Mongols then sacked the city and razed the caliph's palace. They massacred the majority of the city's residents—possibly as many as eight hundred thousand people. The stench of corpses became so great that the Mongol army vacated the city for a while. They then turned their attention to the countryside, completely destroying the irrigation system in the surrounding agricultural lands, making it impossible for Baghdad to recover its prosperity.

After the destruction of Baghdad and its surroundings, the city of fabled wealth that was once considered the center of the universe became nothing more than a provincial capital—which it would remain until the twentieth century—and the caliphate became part of history. According to Albert Hourani, "Although the memory of the caliphate remained, and was recognized by the law books as being the ideal form of Islamic authority," the authority was split between "the ruler who wielded the sword and the 'ulama who guarded the true religion and claimed to speak in the name of the umma."[61]

The destruction of Baghdad and the murder of the last caliph in 1258 mark for many historians the end of the great Islamic Empire. As historian Wilson Bishai observes, the fall of Baghdad "[brought] an end not only to the Abbasid caliphate in Baghdad, but also to the Arab Empire that had ruled over vast areas of the Middle East for over six hundred years."[62]

Although Islam lived on, and even thrived (Hulegu's grandson became a devout Muslim who busied himself building mosques), continuing its spread around the world, the glory that was Baghdad had passed forever.

THE LEGACY OF THE ISLAMIC CIVILIZATION

In the centuries following Baghdad's fall to the Mongols, many of the glories of the golden age of Islam disappeared. No traces of the fabulous palaces of Baghdad remain. Many of the mosques that

A painting depicts Genghis Khan in battle. In 1258 Khan's descendant, a Mongol named Hulegu, attacked and conquered Baghdad.

Although many of the mosques of the empire were razed or converted into churches, some, like this one in Casablanca, survive as testament to the grandeur of Islam's golden age.

were built throughout the old Islamic Empire were either razed or turned into Christian churches. Few traces remain of the fabulous jewels and sumptuous objects commissioned by the caliphs.

However, the intellectual legacy of Islam endures. All through the Western world today, schoolchildren learn to count using Arabic numerals, and learn to add and subtract using zero, which was passed on to the West by Muslim mathematicians. Students study algebra, geometry, and trigonometry that either originated with Arab mathematicians or was recovered by them as they translated texts of the ancient Greeks. They read the works of Plato and Aristotle, which were preserved, translated, and passed on by Muslim scholars. Every day children read stories about powerful genies, magic lamps, flying carpets, and clever young men who first appeared in the literature of Arabia.

The sick are treated in hospitals, a concept originally developed by Muslim physicians. Modern medicine is founded on the works of Greek physicians that were translated and passed to the West by Muslims, and by innovations developed by Muslim physicians and scientists.

Even though to Western eyes the Islamic Empire may seem a distant and exotic part of history, little known and even less understood, its influence is felt in the world every day.

Notes

Introduction: An Empire That Changed the World

1. Albert Hourani, *A History of the Arab Peoples.* Cambridge, MA: Belknap Press of Harvard University Press, 1991, p. 4.

Chapter 1: The Birth of Islam

2. Quoted in Philip K. Hitti, *History of the Arabs,* 10th ed. New York: St. Martin's, 1970, p. 29.

3. F.E. Peters, *Allah's Commonwealth: A History of Islam in the Near East 600–1100 A.D.* New York: Simon and Schuster, 1973, pp. 47–48.

4. Hourani, *A History of the Arab Peoples,* p. 11.

5. Hitti, *History of the Arabs,* p. 26.

6. Quoted in G.E. von Grunebaum, *Classical Islam: A History 600 A.D.–1258 A.D.* Chicago: Aldine, 1970, p. 19.

7. Peters, *Allah's Commonwealth,* p. 43.

8. Quoted in Peters, *Allah's Commonwealth,* p. 52.

9. Quoted in Hourani, *A History of the Arab Peoples,* p. 16.

10. Quoted in Hourani, *A History of the Arab Peoples,* p. 17.

11. Quoted in Hitti, *History of the Arabs,* p. 118.

12. Quoted in Hitti, *History of the Arabs,* p. 120.

Chapter 2: Building the Empire

13. Hitti, *History of the Arabs,* p. 142.

14. Quoted in von Grunebaum, *Classical Islam,* p. 51.

15. Quoted in Hitti, *History of the Arabs,* p. 144.

16. Hitti, *History of the Arabs,* p. 142.

17. Hitti, *History of the Arabs,* p. 149.

18. Quoted in Hitti, *History of the Arabs,* p. 152.

19. Wilson B. Bishai, *Islamic History of the Middle East: Backgrounds, Development, and Fall of the Arab Empire.* Boston: Allyn and Bacon, 1968, p. 144.

20. Quoted in Bishai, *Islamic History of the Middle East,* p. 145.

21. Hitti, *History of the Arabs,* p. 159.

22. Quoted in Hitti, *History of the Arabs,* p. 163.

23. Quoted in Hitti, *History of the Arabs,* p. 165.

24. Peters, *Allah's Commonwealth,* pp. 82–83.

25. Hourani, *A History of the Arab Peoples,* p. 102.

Chapter 3: Governing an Empire: Umar and the Umayyad Dynasty

26. Hitti, *History of the Arabs,* p. 177.

27. Hitti, *History of the Arabs,* p. 183.

28. Hitti, *History of the Arabs,* p. 185.

29. Quoted in Hitti, *History of the Arabs,* p. 197.

30. Quoted in Sayyed Fadhil Bahr-ul-Uloom, "Aspects of the Life of Imam Husayn," http://playandlearn.org/muharram/Muharram2.htm.

31. Hourani, *A History of the Arab Peoples,* p. 27.

32. Hitti, *History of the Arabs,* pp. 285–86.

Chapter 4: The Abbasid Caliphate

33. Quoted in Hourani, *A History of the Arab Peoples,* p. 58.

34. Hourani, *A History of the Arab Peoples,* pp. 43–44.

35. Quoted in Hitti, *History of the Arabs,* pp. 318–19.

36. Hitti, *History of the Arabs,* p. 322.

37. Hitti, *History of the Arabs,* p. 322.

38. Hitti, *History of the Arabs,* p. 329.

Chapter 5: The Golden Age of Islam

39. Von Grunebaum, *Classical Islam,* pp. 80–81.

40. Quoted in Hourani, *A History of the Arab Peoples,* p. 120.

41. Quoted in Hitti, *History of the Arabs,* p. 333.

42. Quoted in Hitti, *History of the Arabs,* p. 334.

43. Quoted in Hourani, *A History of the Arab Peoples*, p. 33.

44. Quoted in Hourani, *A History of the Arab Peoples*, p. 34.

45. Hitti, *History of the Arabs*, p. 420.

46. Quoted in Hourani, *A History of the Arab Peoples*, p. 34.

47. Quoted in *Islam: Empire of Faith*, DVD, directed by Robert Gardner. Gardner Films in association with PBS and Devillier Donegan Enterprises, 2000.

Chapter 6: Intellectual and Artistic Achievements of the Golden Age

48. Hitti, *History of the Arabs*, p. 363.

49. Quoted in IslamiCity, "Islam and Islamic History in Arabia and the Middle East," www.islamicity.com/mosque/ihame/Sec12.htm.

50. Peters, *Allah's Commonwealth*, p. 215.

51. Quoted in Hitti, *History of the Arabs*, p. 347.

Chapter 7: The Rise of Regional Dynasties

52. Hitti, *History of the Arabs*, p. 484.

53. Hitti, *History of the Arabs*, p. 509.

54. Quoted in Hitti, *History of the Arabs*, p. 620.

55. Quoted in Bishai, *Islamic History of the Middle East*, p. 262.

56. P.H. Newby, *Saladin in His Time*. London: Phoenix, 1983, p. 22.

57. Newby, *Saladin in His Time*, p. 22.

58. Quoted in Hitti, *History of the Arabs*, p. 487.

59. Von Grunebaum, *Classical Islam*, p. 200.

60. Hitti, *History of the Arabs*, p. 487.

61. Hourani, *A History of the Arab Peoples*, pp. 143–44.

62. Bishai, *Islamic History of the Middle East*, p. 278.

For Further Reading

Books

George Beshore, *Science in Early Islamic Culture*. New York: Franklin Watts, 1998. Discusses the extraordinary scientific discoveries and advancements in the Islamic world during its golden age and their impact on Western civilization.

Charles Clark, *Islam*. San Diego: Lucent, 2002. Discusses the history, beliefs, popularity, practices, politics, and challenges of one of the world's major religions, Islam.

The Koran. Trans. J.M. Rodwell. London: J.M. Dent & Sons, 1992. Can be sampled to get a sense of the content of Islam's holy book.

P.H. Newby, *Saladin in His Time*. London: Phoenix, 1983. For older readers, an interesting, readable history of Saladin, how he came to power, how he ruled, and how he defeated the European crusaders.

James Rumford, *Traveling Man: The Journey of Ibn Battuta, 1325–1354*. New York: Houghton Mifflin, 2001. Exquisitely illustrated, this brief story of the travels of Ibn Battuta is taken from his own account. Although Ibn Battuta lived in the fourteenth century, the book gives a sense of the expanse and grandeur of the Islamic Empire.

Film

Islam: Empire of Faith, DVD. Directed by Robert Gardner. Gardner Films in association with PBS and Devillier Donegan Enterprises, 2000. Viewers of all ages will appreciate this beautifully filmed and informative overview of the Islamic Empire.

Web Sites

anwary-islam.com (http://anwary-islam.com). This Web site includes information on a wide array of central figures in the history of the Islamic Empire.

Islam: Empire of Faith (www.pbs.org/empires/islam). An accompanying source for the PBS film *Islam: Empire of Faith*. Includes a broad portrait of Islamic art and culture as well as the basic unity of Islamic civilization during its long history.

Islam Guide: A Brief Illustrated Guide to Understanding Islam (www.islamguide.com). A guide to help non-Muslims understand Islam and the Koran.

Works Consulted

Books

Wilson B. Bishai, *Islamic History of the Middle East: Backgrounds, Development, and Fall of the Arab Empire.* Boston: Allyn and Bacon, 1968. A thorough overview of the Islamic Empire through the fall of Baghdad.

Fred McGraw Donner, *The Early Islamic Conquests.* Princeton, NJ: Princeton University Press, 1981. A detailed, scholarly study of Islamic expansion through the conquest of Iraq in the mid-600s.

G.E. von Grunebaum, *Classical Islam: A History 600 A.D.–1258 A.D.* Chicago: Aldine, 1970. A scholarly look at the Islamic world from pre-Islamic times to the fall of Baghdad in 1258.

Philip K. Hitti, *History of the Arabs.* 10th ed. New York: St. Martin's, 1970. A classic study of the Islamic world from pre-Islamic times to the twentieth century. Scholarly but readable, with an abundance of references from primary sources.

———, *The Near East in History: A 5000 Year History.* Princeton, NJ: Van Nostrand, 1961. A readable general history of the Middle East.

Albert Hourani, *A History of the Arab Peoples.* Cambridge, MA: Belknap Press of Harvard University Press, 1991. A learned but readable history of the Muslim world from Muhammad through the mid-1980s.

F.E. Peters, *Allah's Commonwealth: A History of Islam in the Near East 600–1100 A.D.* New York: Simon and Schuster, 1973. A scholarly look at the Islamic world from a primarily religious perspective.

Internet Sources

"Abu Bakr," University of Delaware, http://udel.edu/stu-org/msaud/ISLAM/Bakr.html.

"Abu Bakr, the First Caliph (632–634 C.E.)," 1997. www.cyberistan.org/islamic/abu-bakr.html.

Sayyad Fadhil Bahr-ul-Uloom, "Aspects of the Life of Imam Husayn," http://playandlearn.org/muharram/Muharram2.htm.

Geographia, "The Bedouin Way," www.geographia.com/egypt/sinai/bedouin02.htm.

"Husayn," *Encyclopaedia of the Orient*, http://lexicorient.com/e.o/husayn.htm.

IslamiCity, "Islam and Islamic History in Arabia and the Middle East." www.islamicity.com/mosque/ihama/see12.htm.

———, "The People of 'Ad and Ubar, the Atlantis of the Sands," www.islamicity.com/science/QuranAndScience.

"Rabi'ah al 'Adawiyyah," www.sufimaster.org/adawiyya.htm.

Saudi Arabian Information Resource, "King Fahd's Expansion of the Holy Mosque in Makkah," www.saudinf.com/main/b712.htm.

"Ulama," *Encyclopaedia of the Orient*, http://lexicorient.com/e.o/ulama.htm.

Index

Picture Credits

Cover image: Hamburg
  Kunsthalle, Hamburg,
  Germany/Bridgeman Art
  Library
Archives Charmet/Bridgeman
  Art Library, 73
The Art Archive, 28
The Art Archive/Dagli Orti, 47
The Art Archive/Museum of
  Modern Art Cairo/Dagli Orti,
  52
The Art Archive/Topkapi Muse-
  um Istanbul/HarperCollins
  Publishers, 20
© Art Resource, 60, 69
Bridgeman Art Library, 58, 67,
  72, 76, 97
© Cameraphoto Arte/Art
  Resource, 44
© CORBIS, 80
© Corel Corporation, 84
© Giraudon/Art Resource, 15,
  19, 78

© Chinch Gryniewicz;
  Ecoscene/CORBIS, 98
Hamburg Kunsthalle, Hamburg,
  Germany/Bridgeman Art
  Library, 87
© Hulton/Archive by Getty
  Images, 35
Index/Bridgeman Art Library, 57
© North Wind Pictures, 9, 23, 41,
  64
PhotoDisc, 85
© Réunion des Musées
  Nationaux/Art Resource, 17
© Scala/Art Resource, 13
© SEF/Art Resource, 91
The Stapleton
  Collection/Bridgeman Art
  Library, 26, 54
© Stock Montage, Inc., 95
© Victoria & Albert Museum,
  London/Art Resource, 38
Walters Art Museum, Baltimore,
  USA/Bridgeman Art Library, 83

About the Author

Phyllis Corzine lives in St. Louis, Missouri, and works as a freelance writer of educational materials for elementary and high school students. She has a master's degree in English and American literature from Washington University. Corzine has written several other books for Lucent, including *The French Revolution* (1995), *The Black Death* (1996), *The Palestinian-Israeli Accord* (1997), *The King James Bible: Christianity's Definitive Text* (2000), and *Iraq* (2003). Her other work includes a variety of educational materials, as well as *Eddie's Magic Radio*, a fantasy novel for young adults, and a transliteration into modern English of Shakespeare's *Julius Caesar* for Barron's Educational Series.